THE
ONE
GOD

D1502810

A BOOK OF THE
NEW MESSAGE
FROM GOD

THE
ONE
GOD

AS REVEALED TO
Marshall Vian Summers

THE
ONE
GOD

Copyright © 2016 by The Society for the New Message

All rights reserved. No part of this publication may be reproduced, stored in a retrieval system or transmitted in any form or by any means, electronic, mechanical, photo-copying, recording or otherwise without the prior written permission of the publisher.

Edited by Darlene Mitchell
Cover and interior: Designed by Reed Summers

ISBN: 978-1-942293-10-1
NKL POD Version 7.0
Library of Congress Control Number: 201690558

Publisher's Cataloging-in-Publication
(Provided by Quality Books, Inc.)

Summers, Marshall Vian, author.
   The one God / as revealed to Marshall Vian Summers.
   pages cm
   "A book of the New Message from God."
   LCCN 2016905589
   ISBN 978-1-942293-10-1
   ISBN 978-1-942293-11-8 (ebook)

   1. Society for the New Message--Doctrines.
   2. Spiritual life--Society for the New Message.
   I. Society for the New Message. II. Title.

BP605.S58S8346 2016   299'.93
                                 QBI16-600063

The One God is a book of the New Message from God and is published by New Knowledge Library, the publishing imprint of The Society for the New Message. The Society is a religious non-profit organization dedicated to presenting and teaching a New Message for humanity. The books of New Knowledge Library can be ordered at www.newknowledgelibrary.org, your local bookstore and at many other online retailers.

The New Message is being studied in more than 20 languages in over 90 countries. *The One God* is being translated into the many languages of our world by a dedicated group of volunteer student translators from around the world. These translations will all be available online at www.newmessage.org.

The Society for the New Message
P.O. Box 1724   Boulder, CO 80306-1724
(303) 938-8401   (800) 938-3891
011 303 938 84 01 (International)   (303) 938-1214 (fax)
newmessage.org   newknowledgelibrary.org
email: society@newmessage.org

*W*e shall speak of God, the Higher Authority.

―――――――――

*T*he Higher Authority is speaking to you now,
speaking through the Angelic Presence,
speaking to a part of you that is the very center
and source of your Being.

―――――――――

*T*he Higher Authority has a Message for the world
and for each person in the world.

―――――――――

*T*he Higher Authority is calling to you, calling to you down
through the Ancient Corridors of your mind,
calling to you beyond your beliefs and your preoccupations.

―――――――――

*F*or God has spoken again and
the Word and the Sound are in the world.

From *God Has Spoken Again*
Chapter 3: The Engagement

THE ONE GOD

TABLE OF CONTENTS

INTRODUCTION

The One God is a book of Revelation given by the Creator of all life to the human family through the Messenger Marshall Vian Summers.

Here God is revealing the greater reality of the Divine Presence, both in our world and within a Greater Community of intelligent life in the universe. This opens the next chapter in the progressive Revelation of God's Reality, Will and Purpose for the human family as it now stands at the threshold of great change and instability in the world.

Throughout human history, the Creator has given Revelation and Wisdom to meet the growing needs of people and nations at great turning points in the evolution of humanity. Through the Prophets, Messengers and revealed Teachings of the past, God's progressive Revelations have flowed into human awareness, advancing our understanding of the One God and re-awakening a deep memory of the Divine Presence in our lives.

Now God is speaking again, delivering a New Revelation to meet the critical and escalating needs of a global humanity, now facing Great Waves of environmental, political and economic change and the world's emergence into a greater panorama of intelligent life in the universe. To face and navigate this future, we need a New Message from God, for the great traditions of the past cannot prepare us for the thresholds before us.

God's progressive Revelation continues anew through a New Message from God, of which *The One God* is but a small part. The words of this text are a direct communication from God, translated into human language by the Angelic Presence that watches over this world, and then spoken through the Messenger Marshall Vian Summers, who has given over 30 years of his life to this process of Revelation.

The One God is the second book of Volume 1 of the New Message from God. *The One God* contains 12 individual revelations, each given at different times and places during the Messenger's journeys in the world. The Messenger has now compiled these revelations into this united text.

The One God is a book of many teachings. It teaches us to go beyond our concepts and beliefs about God in order to explore our own experience of the presence and mystery of the Divine reality in our lives. It teaches us that, both in our world and throughout the universe, God redeems the separated through Knowledge—the spiritual intelligence and power that God has placed within each of us to guide, protect and lead us to a greater life of purpose and relationship.

The One God opens a new vantage point from which to see ourselves and the world in which we live as never before. From this new vantage point, we can glimpse back into the origins of the universe and gain a new understanding of the great Separation from God that gave rise to the evolution of all life and that ultimately explains our presence in the world at this time. With this, *The One God* offers us a unique experience and remembrance of the timeless state of Creation, from which we have all come and to which we will all return.

This represents a new experience of God. Instead of being focused or fixated on pleasing God, fearing God, talking to God, fighting for God or running from God, we are invited into a new and deeper engagement with the mysterious Presence of the Creator and the power of Knowledge that the Creator has given us.

In the end, *The One God* teaches that the greater reality and purpose of God is beyond the beliefs, concepts and definitions of any person, scripture or religion. Rather, God is now revealed as a timeless experience available to you and to all people—people of all religions and of no religion. God is an experience of remembrance, a remembrance of the Greater Reality from which we have come and to which we will return eventually. Here we find an intimate form of redemption—redemption from a life of separation, pain and confusion. Here we can begin to experience who we really are, where we have come from and why we are in the world at this time.

Though it appears to be a book in the hand, *The One God* is something far greater. It is a calling and a communication from the Heart of God to you. In the pages of this book, God's Presence calls to you and to all people, calling for you to awaken from the dream and the nightmare of living in Separation apart from your Source, calling down through the Ancient Corridors of your mind to the spiritual presence and power that live within you, waiting to be discovered.

The One God is part of a living communication from God to humanity. Remarkably, you have found the New Message from God, or it has found you. It is no coincidence that this is the case. This opens the next chapter in the mystery of your life and of your presence in the world at this time. The door opens before you. You need only enter to begin.

As you enter more deeply into the Revelation, the impact on your life will grow, bringing a greater experience of clarity, inner certainty and true direction to your life. In time, your questions will be answered as you find growing freedom from self-doubt, inner conflict and the restraints of the past. Here *the One God* is speaking to you directly, revealing to you the greater life that you were always destined to live.

New Knowledge Library

ABOUT THE NEW MESSAGE
FROM GOD

*T*he New Message from God is a living communication from the Creator of all life to the heart of every man, woman and child on Earth. This communication is here to ignite the spiritual power of humanity, to sound God's calling for unity amongst the world's nations and religions and to prepare humanity for a radically changing world and for its destiny in a larger universe of intelligent life.

The New Message from God is the largest Revelation ever given to humanity, given now to a literate world of global communication and growing global awareness. It is not given for one tribe, one nation or one religion alone, but instead to reach the entire world, a world very different from the ancient world of the former Messengers. Never before has there been a Divine Revelation of this depth and magnitude, given by God to all people of the world in the lifetime of the Messenger.

The New Message from God has not entered the world through the existing religious authorities and institutions of today. It has not come to the leaders of religion or to those who garner fame and recognition.

Instead, God's New Message has entered the world as it has always done. It has come quietly, unlooked for and unannounced, given to a humble man chosen and sent into the world for this one task, to be a Messenger for humanity at this great turning point.

At the center of the New Message from God is the original Voice of Revelation, which has spoken the words of every book of the New Message. Never before has the Voice of Revelation, the Voice that spoke to the Messengers and Prophets of the past, been recorded in its original purity and made available to each person to hear and to experience for themselves. In this way, the Word and the Sound are in the world.

In this remarkable process of spoken Revelation, the Presence of God communicates beyond words to the Angelic Assembly that oversees the world. The Assembly then translates this communication into human language and speaks all as one through their Messenger, whose voice becomes the vehicle for this greater Voice—the Voice of Revelation.

The words of this Voice were recorded in audio form, transcribed and are now made available in the books of the New Message. In this way, the purity of God's original spoken Message is preserved and given to all people in the world.

The Messenger has walked a long and difficult road to bring The New Message from God to you and to the world. The process of Revelation began in 1981 and continues to this day.

At this time, The Messenger is engaged in compiling over three decades of spoken Revelation into a final and complete testament— The One Book of the New Message from God. This new testament will be divided into six volumes and possibly more. Each volume will contain two or more books, and each book will be organized into chapters and verses. Therefore, the New Message from God will be structured in the following way: Volume > Book > Chapter > Verse.

In order to bring this spoken communication into written form, slight textual and grammatical adjustments were made by the Messenger. This was requested of him by the Angelic Assembly to aid the understanding of the reader and to convey the Message according to the grammatical standards of the written English language.

In some instances, the Messenger has inserted a word not originally spoken in the Revelation. When present, you will often find this inserted word in brackets. Consider these bracketed insertions as direct clarifications by the Messenger, placed in the text by him alone in order to ensure that ambiguities in the spoken communication do not cause confusion or incorrect interpretations of the text.

In some cases, the Messenger has removed a word to aid the readability of the text. This was usually done in the case of certain conjunctions, articles, pronouns and prepositions that made the text awkward or grammatically incorrect.

The Messenger alone has made these slight changes and only to convey the original spoken communication with the greatest clarity possible. None of the original meaning or intention of the communication has been altered.

The text of this book has been structured by the Messenger into verse. Each verse roughly signals the beginning or ending of a distinct topic or message point communicated by the Source.

The verse structure of the text allows the reader to access the richness of the content and those subtle messages that may otherwise be missed in longer paragraphs of text that convey multiple topics. In this way, each topic and idea communicated by the Source is given its own standing, allowing it to speak from the page directly to the reader. The Messenger has determined that structuring the text in verse is the most efficacious and faithful way of rendering the original spoken revelations of the New Message.

The rendering of this text is according to the Messenger's original will and intention. Here we are privileged to witness the process of preparation and compilation being undertaken by the Messenger, in his own time, by his own hands. This process stands in stark contrast to the fact that the former great traditions were largely not put into written form by their Messengers, leaving the original messages vulnerable to alteration and corruption over time.

Here the Messenger seals in purity the texts of God's New Message and gives them to you, to the world and to all people in the future. Whether this book is opened today or 500 years from now, God's original communication will speak from these pages with the same intimacy, purity and power as on the day it was spoken.

CHAPTER 1

COMPREHENDING GOD

As revealed to
Marshall Vian Summers
on January 31, 2007
in Boulder, Colorado

It is time now for a greater comprehension of God and an expanded understanding of God, who is the Source and Author of your life and of all life within this world and throughout the Greater Community of worlds in which you live.

This new understanding is not to correct previous understanding as much as it is to expand it, to make it more complete, to leave the door open for a greater experience of the Divine Will and Presence in your life.

In presenting a New Message from God, it is necessary then to renew this experience, to freshen it, to separate it from all the things that have been added by human institutions and human inventions, to bring it into greater focus and clarity for you.

Here it is important not to confuse God with religion, for many terrible things have been done in the name of religion and in the name of God. But God exists far beyond all of these things—far beyond human error, far beyond human imagination, far beyond human invention and far beyond human corruption.

It is necessary now for you to consider God within the larger arena of intelligent life in which you live, which includes all life within this world, but extends beyond it into the Greater Community [the universe].

To have a pure experience of the Divine Reality and the Divine Will for your life, you must gain this Greater Community understanding of God.

Otherwise, you will think of God as a projection of your own personality, as a projection of your own emotions, thoughts and feelings. You will project onto God your anger, your preferences, your judgments, whatever sense of revenge you might have, your notions of justice and punishment and so forth.

But God exists beyond all of this—the real God, the pure God that has been shining like the sun upon you. Regardless of the clouds in the sky, regardless of the pollution in the atmosphere and the turbulence on the ground, God is like the sun shining upon you.

But God is beyond the sun, beyond any definition that you can make. Beyond your histories, beyond the great teachers and the great Messengers from God, beyond the great spiritual books and testimonies, there is God the Creator and the Author of your life and existence.

What God has created in you lives within you now. It lives beyond your intellect, beyond your thoughts and understanding, beyond your concepts, beyond your ideas and beliefs in a deeper place within you—a deeper mind, a mind that in the New Message is called Knowledge. It is the mind that knows. It is the mind that waits. It is the mind that sees clearly without distortion, without fear, without preference, without confusion, without speculation—a deeper mind within you.

This is what God has created in you that is permanent, that will last forever. Beyond your temporary identity in this world, beyond all the events of this world and all other worlds, beyond the river of your experience in this life, there is Knowledge within you, and it is God that is the Author of this Knowledge.

If you think of God within this greater context, you can begin to appreciate the power and magnificence of God's Creation, in the world and eventually within yourself.

Your body, your mind, your personality—these are all temporary vehicles whose greater purpose is to express your relationship with God and the Wisdom that God has given to you to communicate and to contribute to a world in need.

Think then of your mind, your body, your intellect as vehicles of expression, valuable in and of themselves, but not as valuable as that which they are meant to express and to serve.

Then you will begin to see that God permeates all things, lives within all things and yet is beyond all things—all at the same time.

You can feel this Presence wherever you are, and you can find and follow Knowledge wherever you are.

Therefore, to fully understand and experience God within your life, you must come to Knowledge within yourself, which is the Greater Intelligence, the permanence that God has created within you and for you. It is who you really are, beyond all concepts, ideas and delusions. It is your true nature.

It is by gaining a connection with Knowledge, by learning to discern Knowledge and to follow Knowledge that you learn to experience the Presence, the Power and the Will of God in your life.

Beyond this, God remains forever beyond the concepts of the intellect, beyond all human inventions, beyond all individual and collective philosophies. For what set of ideas or concepts can contain a God of the Greater Community, the Author of countless races of beings, all unique and different from one another in so many ways?

To come to God then is to come to Knowledge within yourself, for this is what calls you to God. Perhaps you will be called to a certain place or to a certain person, but it is for this purpose—to experience the Presence within yourself. For you will need more than belief to appreciate, comprehend and follow what God has given you to see, to know and to do.

Let this then be the starting place for you, where you take the Steps to Knowledge, where you take the steps to God. And you do this whether you are a Christian, a Buddhist or a Muslim. Whatever faith tradition you adhere to, or even if you do not have a faith tradition, there are still the Steps to Knowledge.

Knowledge is what created all the world's religions, and Knowledge is what unites them still, despite all of the separation and conflict that exist between them. For these are a human invention and not a Divine invention.

The Calling reverberates through all of these traditions—within them and beyond them. It is a Calling that sounds throughout the universe to return to the power and presence of Knowledge, to discover what

Knowledge has for you to do, to see and to know. This initiates the return—the Calling, the listening, the responding and the return.

Let this be your understanding.

CHAPTER 2

THE NEW GOD

As revealed to
Marshall Vian Summers
on February 12, 2009
in Boulder, Colorado

There is a New Revelation about God, a Revelation that takes God out of the ancient history of humanity, out of the conflicts and the fantasies and the misunderstanding of humanity. This Revelation takes God into the larger panorama of life in the universe called the Greater Community.

You need this new understanding of God now because the God of the ancients was a small God, a God of your world and of your time, a God of your cultures, a God of your people in ancient time.

But humanity has outgrown this God, this human God, this angry God, this vengeful God, this God that seems to be a projection of your personality and tendencies.

It is not that the ancients were wrong; it is just that their comprehension was limited. It is not that they created a God in their own likeness; it is that they could not comprehend a God that was beyond their likeness.

The New Revelation presents God within a greater context, within the context of intelligent life in the universe. This is not a human context, for it is not a human universe that you are facing.

It is not a God that is preoccupied with this one world alone. It is not a God that judges the way that you would judge or condemns the way that you would condemn. It is not a God that needs praise and worship, that must have obedience and adulation. That is the old God of the tribe. That is the old God that favors one nation over another, one people over another. That is an old idea of God.

But God has never been like this, you see. For the God that people have looked to and have worshipped, the God that people have apprehended and misapprehended has always been the God of the Greater Community—the vast expanses of space, other dimensions of reality and countless races of beings so different from the human family.

This is the one God of the universe—not a God of one world, one people or one tribe; not a God that thinks, acts or behaves the way that human beings think, act and behave.

This God is not limited to one Revelation for humanity, for there have been successive Revelations for humanity. And now there is a New Revelation for humanity to prepare the human family for the great change that is coming to the world and to prepare humanity for its future, destiny and encounter with a Greater Community of intelligent life in the universe.

It will not be possible for you to think of God in the old ways if you want to understand God's New Revelation for the world. You will not be able to understand the reality and the significance of intelligent life in the universe if you think of God in old ways.

For the old God was exclusive to humanity—a God of one nation, a God of one people, a God of one race, a God of one world alone.

That is why the old God was too limited and too much discerned in the likeness of humanity alone to comprehend God's real nature and purpose, even here in this world.

The old God took people to war. The old God seemed to have no concern for the welfare of people and nations that God did not favor. The old God was used by kings, monarchs and nations to justify and to amplify their nation's grievances and ambitions.

The old God seemed to delight in punishing humanity for the inevitable errors that humanity would make in its separated state living in this world.

And so the whole notion of Heaven and Hell is built around the belief and the assumptions about the old God.

But the new God, the God of the Greater Community, the God of a greater reality than your own, requires a redefinition of all of these things. For God's reality is so very different from how God has been considered and believed in, in the past.

God does not favor one nation over another. God does not lead peoples to war. God does not will one nation's victory over another nation or one people's conquest of another people.

God does not will for natural disasters, plagues, illness, catastrophe. You can blame these things on the old God, but not on the new God. For God has set in motion the forces of nature, evolution and geologic change at the beginning of time, and that is all running itself now.

God is intelligent. God does not have to run every little thing. God does not have to move the blood through your veins or operate your millions of cells. God does not have to run the weather of the world.

God does not have to run the nations of the world, the economies of the world. It is all set in motion. It was set in motion at the beginning of time.

But God watches over the world and all worlds—calling to the separated to return, calling through the avenues of religion, calling through the avenues of conscience, calling through the avenues of true love and recognition.

The God of the universe does not care what your religious beliefs are so long as they can assist you in bringing you to the deeper Knowledge that God has placed within you—a deeper intelligence that God has placed within you to guide you, to protect you and to lead you to a greater service and contribution in the world.

The old God was dominated by religious institutions. If you did not support those institutions and believe in their ideology, it was considered you would be sent to Hell, that you were affronting God. But God does not care about these things.

The beliefs and fascinations, obsessions and fantasies of humanity are not what move God. It is the deeper movement of the heart and the conscience. It is the act of selfless giving. It is the act of forgiveness and the desire to contribute beyond one's own personal needs and preferences. It is the recognition of one to another. It is an enemy becoming a friend. It is the healing of the natural world that has been despoiled. These are the things that move the Lord of the universe.

If you are to understand humanity's destiny and future within a Greater Community of life in the universe, if you are to understand how to prepare for the Great Waves of change that are coming to the world, then you must have a new experience and understanding of the Divine.

If you cling to the old ideas, the old definitions, you will not understand what humanity is facing and how to prepare. You will think it is the end of time. You will think it is the great punishment. You will think it is the final battle—all these kinds of things that seem to indicate a grand finale to the human experience.

But humanity is but leaving one stage of its development and entering another. It is a great transition from a world of tribal societies and warring factions to a more united and powerful humanity—a humanity that can live, function and remain free within a Greater Community of life; a humanity that can face intervention from other races in the universe and can establish its own rules of engagement here; a united humanity that can learn to live within the boundaries and limited resources of this world, without driving it into oblivion and decline.

A united humanity will need a new experience and understanding of the Divine if it is to make this great transition and to avoid the ever-growing temptation towards conflict, competition and war. Facing a world of declining resources, a world of environmental disruption, a world of violent weather and growing economic instability, you will need to have a greater experience of the Divine and particularly of the power of Knowledge within yourself. For it is at this deeper level beneath the surface of your intellect that God will touch you and move you, by the very force of attraction of the Divine.

You cannot comprehend God with your intellect. You cannot reduce God down into a rational principle. You must see that God is not operating all the functions of the world, for these were set in motion at the beginning of time.

There is no conflict here between Creation and evolution. There is really no conflict between religion and science. They are all born out of the same reality, the same needs to comprehend life, the same needs to correct human error and to establish a safe and secure future for the human family.

Religion and science are corrupted by the same forces—the desire for individual power, the domination of one group over another, institutions fighting for supremacy. They are both orthodox in their own right and both tend to be limited and self-defensive.

Instead of trying to connect the past with the present and the future, it is best to let the past go, to see that humanity's understanding of the Divine is an evolutionary process in and of itself. If you try to connect the future with the past, you will either deny the future or you will have to change your understanding of the past.

Ancient prophecies will not be fulfilled. The messiah will not return to the world. It is now the time for Knowledge to emerge. It is the era of human cooperation and human responsibility. No one great leader is going to come and lead humanity into a glorious future. No one individual is going to come and settle all the scores and take revenge upon the wicked. That is the old idea of God. It is no longer relevant, and it was never really true to begin with. It is the desire of people for a final resolution to the conundrum of life, to the questions of life, to the problem of life.

You were sent into the world to make a contribution here, a specific contribution concerning certain people in certain situations. Do not think that you understand these yet. Do not yet assume that you are fully involved in these yet.

Do not think that by believing in a religious ideology that you are going to be saved. For if you do not do what you came here to do, if you do not engage with those who you are meant to engage with and to contribute your gifts, belief alone will not bridge the gap and end the Separation between you and God.

To reunite with God, you have to become more like what God really created in you. God has placed Knowledge within you to guide you and to redeem you. Beliefs are secondary and often stand in the way of this redemption.

Thinking that your religion is the one true religion will stand in the way of your redemption. Condemning other nations, peoples and religions will prevent you from receiving this redemption. Being self-righteous and the defender of your faith will blind you, and you will turn your back to God.

You must have the courage and the faith in the Divine to think of God anew, to realize your responsibilities here and to recognize that you were sent into the world to be a contributor, not a judge or a critic.

Here you must realize that God has initiated all the world's religions and they have all been changed by people, even radically changed. So to correct the errors of the past, to renew the true faith and to bring forth the great truth of the ancient religions in their pure form, God has sent a New Revelation into the world, not to replace the religions of the world, but to clarify them and to give them new strength and power and a greater unity with one another.

It is not just a correction, however; it is a preparation for a future that will be unlike the past. You are facing a non-human universe. You are facing environmental destruction and ever-growing instability and insecurity in the world. You are facing a world of declining resources, a world where an ever-growing population will have to drink from a slowly shrinking well. You may pray to God to save you, but God has sent you here to save the world, to play your small but essential part in this.

It is not the end of time. It is a great transition. It is not the end of the world. It is a great reckoning and a new time of Revelation.

Many things will come to an end. Many ways of life will have to be altered. Human understanding will have to change. Human responsibility will have to grow. Human compassion will have to grow. Human forgiveness will have to grow. It will seem like the end of time, like the whole world is coming down on you, a time of cataclysmic change and upheaval. But it is really a time for humanity to grow up, to become wise and to prepare for its future.

Only God knows what is coming over the horizon, and only God can prepare you for this completely. You may recognize certain solutions to aspects of the world's problems, but you cannot prepare yourself for the Great Waves of change or for your encounter with intelligent life in the universe.

God has sent a New Revelation into the world to prepare humanity for its future, to warn humanity of the great dangers within the world and beyond the world and to bless humanity with the power and the presence of Knowledge that has been placed as a deeper strength within each person so that humanity will choose peace over war, cooperation over division, resolution over the loss of confidence, freedom over capitulation and responsibility over weakness.

This is not the providence of a few inspired individuals or a few small groups working to support the human family. It will have to be something that will have to reach far and wide. Not everyone will have to receive and believe in the New Message from God, but it must reach enough people to have its impact here, to provide a new awareness and experience of the Divine in your life and the deeper movement of your life.

Here you will have to let go of your notions of Heaven and Hell, your belief in a final Judgment Day and all of these things, for they will not fit with the greater reality that you are entering.

If you follow Knowledge, you will become closer to God. If you deny Knowledge and follow your fears and ambitions, you will become further away from God. If you contribute your gifts in the world, you will not need to come here again. You will have completed this cycle of your evolution and development.

God is not going to just bring you back to Heaven. God is going to put you to work in the universe, in the reality of the separated. You have many present tasks and many future tasks. You do not run away from these into Heaven, for there is much work to do, you see. God does not waste this opportunity. Your redemption must be a source of inspiration for others and must continue to have a resonating and positive effect on life in the universe.

No one will be sent to Hell. But people are already living in Hell, being separated from God—the Hell of their own fearful imagination, the Hell of their self-hatred and hatred of others, the Hell of their circumstances, the Hell of their isolation. Yes, there are worse Hells than this, but God will not send you there.

But if you are left out of God's Grace and Power, God's Providence and God's Guidance, then your Hell will deepen and can seem to be endless. But it is not endless, for God has placed Knowledge within you, and eventually you will come to realize that you must follow this Knowledge, you must accept this Knowledge and that only

Knowledge can take you from the Hell of your Separation, from your isolation and from your own grievances and self-denial.

In the end, God will win everyone back, even the most wicked. They will just have to work longer to redeem themselves; they will have to give more to counteract their harmful impacts upon others. Here kings will have to be water carriers and till the fields. Here tyrants will have to sweep the streets.

People are impatient. They want a Judgment Day; they want everything to be finished. They do not want to have to live with great questions, great unresolved questions. They want God to punish others that they themselves cannot or will not punish. They think they know what justice is.

That is why the old God is filled with revenge and anger and repudiation, that people are forced to believe with the threat of death and Hell. That is a primitive way of looking at life. It is an ignorant way of looking at life. It does not account for the reality of the Divine or the reality of your Divine nature and destiny.

God will call everyone back eventually, but eventually could be a long time from now. In the interim you suffer; you live in darkness and confusion. You do not realize your power, your value or the greater strength of Knowledge within you that is waiting to be discovered and that is trying to save you, even at this moment.

If humanity is to escape great collapse in the future, if you are to escape domination by other races from the universe, you must now listen and gain a new and greater understanding of the Divine Presence and Power in your life, the real nature of human destiny and what will be required of peoples, groups and nations to choose wisely in the face of a changing world.

Here your old beliefs are clarified and purified. Here you do not abandon the great traditions. Instead, you see their connection with one another, and the great value and wisdom that is at the very heart of their teaching.

But your cosmology will change because you are entering the Greater Community. Your religion now cannot be a religion of one world alone or one people alone. It will have to be a Greater Community religion with a God of the universe, and a spirituality of the universe, that which unites you and connects you with one another despite your differing views and interpretations.

Fight against this and you fight against God's Will and Purpose for humanity. Repudiate this and you repudiate your future, your evolution and the primary education you must receive at this time. Lash out against God's New Revelation and you will further distance yourself from the Power and Presence of God in your life.

They are all connected, these Revelations. But you must see their pure thread and content to understand this.

So much of what people believe in is purely a human creation—the stories, the miracles, the traditions of stories and miracles—a human creation. That God created the world in a few days [is] a human creation, the attempt by a limited understanding to comprehend the reality and the mystery of Creation. It is like asking a five-year-old to talk about the evolution of the world. They can only do it with simple language, simple stories and a simple timeframe. They cannot yet comprehend the expanse, the immensity and complexity of what they are looking at.

So as you expand your awareness and your understanding, you gain a greater comprehension of the Divine, the miracle of Creation and the even greater miracle of redemption.

Here the new God is the old God unveiled, clarified, not clothed in ancient understandings or ancient mythologies. For there is only one God and that is God of all the universes, a God of all the races. God has a Plan of redemption for each one, and each one is reclaimed through Knowledge, for God has put Knowledge in each one.

And though most races in the universe are far less free than humanity is at this time—many races are suffering under subjugation by other races, or have become entirely secular and technological in their emphasis—there is still a Plan of redemption for them all.

But can you say what this is? Of course not. Can you define God's Will and Plan for the universe? Of course not. Can you even comprehend a Greater Community of intelligent life—a billion, billion, billion races and many more beyond this?

Here instead of trying to make life fit into your ideology, to make everything squeeze into your limited understanding, you begin to follow the power and the presence of Knowledge within you. That reveals God's Presence and Plan for your life. And you realize that beyond the intellect, there is a greater dimension to your existence and that the intellect must serve this.

Here you cease to proclaim that you know God's Will, and you become humble, and you allow God's Will for you and for this time to be revealed. And if your intention is pure, you will follow something without coming to great conclusions, without proclaiming yourself, without formulating a new ideology that is really a human creation.

Knowledge knows where you are going. Knowledge knows what is coming over the horizon. Knowledge is trying to protect and prepare you even at this moment. But you are not yet aware of the power and presence of Knowledge within yourself sufficiently to hear its messages, to heed its warnings and to receive its guidance. That is why God's New Revelation provides the Steps to Knowledge, so that you can gain access to this deeper reality and this deeper current of your life.

Humanity cannot save itself now. It cannot come up with one solution for the Great Waves of change. It does not know how to prepare itself for a universe of intelligent life—a competitive environment on a scale you cannot even imagine. That is why there is a New Message from God in the world—to provide the Revelation, to provide the warning, to provide the encouragement and to provide the preparation.

Here you must become a person who can function in the Greater Community, a person who can think in terms of the whole world, a person who is not limited and constrained by a previous understanding that is far too limited and insufficient to enable you to perceive your changing circumstances and the great challenges that are coming.

Here the New Revelation opens doors, expands your awareness and perception, liberates you from old ideas that will never allow you to see the present and the future, to free you from condemnation and to bring back to you the mystery and the power of your life and greater purpose in the world.

God has a Greater Plan for the human family, but this Plan can only be followed individually through Knowledge, through cooperation and recognition between peoples, through environmental responsibility, through accountability to the human family, through humility and simplicity without arrogance, without condemnation, without self-righteousness. For these are all a human invention.

And they are not limited to humanity alone. Such tendencies exist throughout the universe. It is the result of Separation, the great Separation from God that set in motion the creation and the expansion of the physical universe. The physical universe is but a small part of God's Creation.

But this remains for you to learn. You have a greater journey and destiny to take here. But you will have to allow your mind to expand, your eyes to open and your ears to hear if you are to gain this greater preparation and understanding.

The old religions, if they are held in contempt of one another, have really become obsolete and will become increasingly so in the future. Now you must see Jesus within the Greater Community, and Muhammad and the Buddha and all the great saints and emissaries in a larger context—within a greater series of Revelations, each bringing humanity closer to world civilization, and to greater cooperation and a deeper experience of the conscience that God has placed within you. In this sense, all religions are ecumenical; they are all meant to support one another instead of compete and denounce one another.

God's Will is for humanity to unite, to preserve the world and to prepare for its future in a Greater Community—a future where humanity's freedom will be challenged repeatedly, a future where humanity will be seduced by the offers of alien technology, a future with many hazards, but a future where humanity must maintain human freedom and sovereignty within this world. Lose this and you lose everything—all the accomplishments of humanity.

Only God's New Revelation can show you these things, for they were not part of God's previous Revelations. For humanity did not need to know of the Greater Community, and humanity was not facing a world in decline in previous eras.

But now you are facing these things, and you must prepare. And that is why an emissary was sent into the world bringing a New Message from God. He is not a savior. He is not magnificent. He is simple and humble. And he is the Messenger.

So once again humanity is challenged with a New Revelation. Can it receive this? Can it comprehend this? Can it accept this, or will it fight and struggle and denounce and continue its violent and ignorant ways? Will the human intellect still try to replace the power of Knowledge within the individual? Will religion grow and expand, or will it contract and become self-defensive?

Will people be able to change, to have a real change of heart to prepare them for the future and to assure them a greater life and a greater security in the world? These are questions that only people can answer.

But the Revelation is upon you because the great needs are upon you. And God has more to say to the human family and has provided a New Revelation and a new way forward.

This has come from the new God, new only to your understanding. For there is only one God, and that God is neither new nor old, but has always been. It is humanity's understanding that must evolve now, and a New Revelation has been given to make this possible.

The Revelation was given in the face of great necessity, for humanity is not recognizing the Great Waves of change and is not responding to the presence of forces from the Greater Community, who are in the world to take advantage of a weak and divided humanity. Humanity is not responding and cannot prepare itself in time, and that is why the Revelation has been given.

It is also being given to uplift humanity's understanding of its spiritual nature and reality to the level of Knowledge, where there are no conflicts and contentiousness between peoples. For Knowledge cannot be in opposition to itself, and your greater spiritual reality and identity were created in harmony with all others. It is only the arrogance of human presumption and the overriding presence of fear and competition that drive people away from their true nature and purpose here.

But be of good cheer, for a great Message is being sent into the world from the Creator of all life in the universe. Have greater confidence, for the power and presence of Knowledge is within you. As you learn to take the Steps to Knowledge, you will find its power, grace and guidance for yourself and for others. And you will see that you truly were created by God and sent into the world for a greater purpose, and that you have a greater destiny beyond this world, and a greater future within and beyond the boundaries of time.

CHAPTER 3

THE ORIGIN

As revealed to
Marshall Vian Summers
on November 18, 2009
in London, England

Life had an origin long ago, before this world existed, before life as you know it existed in this world, before you took form and became an individual in this world.

Life existed with no alternative to life, complete, whole, engaged, all of Creation, magnificent, beyond words and expression, life in the purest form in myriad expressions, creative but harmonious, life that still exists within you at this moment, deep beneath the surface of your mind.

But there was a Separation, and the Separation created the manifest universe that your senses report to you. As there could be no alternative to Creation, God created the manifest universe for all sentient beings who would choose Separation—a place to live, to learn and to taste the small pleasures and the great difficulty of living apart from Creation.

God set in motion the biological and geological forces that have given rise to an expanding universe, a universe full of countless life forms and forms of intelligent life, evolving, but also returning. For in the end, there can be no alternative to Creation.

From where you stand, there seems to be no alternative to manifest life, and Creation seems a very distant and ephemeral reality. The Creator created physical life for the separated to inhabit this universe. It took eons of time, in your sense of time, to create the environment where sentient life could enter into this arena. For time is nothing to God, and everything to you.

The worlds in the universe that this sentient life would inhabit would be livable and habitable, but difficult, for Separation is difficult. Now you would have to learn to constantly solve the problems of survival and provision and contention and conflict with others—others of your own kind and form and others of a very different kind and form. Separation would not be blissful or easy. It would be problematic. Yes, it would have its great pleasures, but they would be short lived, for there is no [permanent} alternative to Creation.

The physical universe is an alternative to Creation, and that is why it is changing and moving, for it has a beginning, a middle and an end. You are somewhere in the middle in the great span of Creation.

Only a very small part of Creation is involved in manifest life. But to you, of course, it is immense and incomprehensible, as it should be. It is not possible for your intellect to comprehend the scope and the magnitude of this.

But there are certain important things for you to realize about your life in the world at this time—why you are here and, most importantly, what lives within you at this moment that connects you with Creation as it really is and as it has always been.

You have no origin really because you are a part of Creation. An origin would only be meaningful within the context of time and in the context of form. But you originate beyond time and form, and so in essence you have no origin. Because you have no origin, you have no end point. That part of you that is eternal and complete, that resides in a deeper part of your mind, lives in this reality.

So now you have two minds. You have the mind of the world, conditioned by the world and influenced by the world, a mind that is full of the world's impressions and influences, and your own responses and decisions in the face of it. But the deeper mind is still connected to Creation.

In God's New Revelation, this is called Knowledge—Knowledge here meaning the deeper mind, the mind that is not part of Separation. The difference between this deeper mind and your surface or worldly mind is the difference between Creation and Separation. You could not separate from God completely. The part of you that did not separate represents Knowledge. The part of you that did separate represents your soul.

Now you are in the world, where you appear to be distinct, an individual, creative, but without a real foundation, alone and struggling to make associations, facing a world of immense difficulty, now having to solve the problems of existence in this state.

But because Knowledge is with you and in you, you are here for a mission. Only Knowledge knows what it is, how it can be achieved and who it will involve.

How different this is from your ideas, your notions and your beliefs about what this could possibly be. Yes, perhaps you sense there is something greater about your life, there is something permanent about your Being and your existence, that you have an existence before this life and beyond this life.

Yet beyond this simple recognition, the mind cannot go, the worldly mind. It cannot reach that far forward or that far back because it only understands those things that are in form and in motion. The truth that you have no origin and no end point is entirely beyond its reasoning capabilities.

No matter what you think you are, no matter what the makeup of your worldly mind or how you identify yourself with places, people and things, the greater association lives within you.

This, then, is your hope and your destiny, your promise of fulfillment and redemption. It is not altered by the world. It is not corrupted by the world. It is not diminished by the world. The world constrains the power and the presence of Knowledge and limits its expression here, but not its reality.

There is no conflict between Creation and evolution, for God created evolution so that everyone in Separation could find their way back. Even the most sinful, the most dreadful and the most depraved will find their way back because there is no alternative to Creation. Even Hell and all the dimensions of Hell that you could possibly imagine are only temporary in the greater scheme of things.

The power, the draw and the calling of God are within you, deep beneath the surface of your mind. With this is the memory of the greater purpose that you are born with, which is not a purpose for Separation, but a purpose for contribution, which has the power to undo your Separation and to liberate you from it, thus returning to you the strength, the confidence and the reality that you are not alone.

You are in the world for a purpose now, not your purpose, but a purpose that was given to you before you came, a purpose that is related to these times and to the Great Waves of change that are coming to the world.

You can pretend. You can remain self-obsessed. You can occupy every moment of every day and dream through every night, but you are really running away from this greater purpose and from the power and the calling of God within you.

When We speak of the origin, We are speaking of that which has a beginning, a middle and an end. The origin of your physical existence in this life has a beginning, a middle and an end. The origin of your nation has a beginning, a middle and an end. The origin of this world as a physical place has a beginning, a middle and an end, though in the scope of time this is very long. Even the universe that you perceive as far as your eyes and ears and touch can reach, it too has a beginning, a middle and an end.

This is the theology of the Greater Community, the theology of all life in the universe, not simply the theology of one little race in one little world.

It is being given to humanity now because humanity is emerging into this Greater Community of life and is facing the grave danger that is posed by the Great Waves of change—environmental collapse in the world and all of the problems that that will create for the human family.

That is why a New Revelation has to be given, not only to prepare you for the Great Waves of change, but to begin to educate you about the nature of spirituality in the universe and the larger picture of your existence so that you can find your place within a far greater reality.

There is no one on Earth who could give you this theology, for there is no one on Earth who understands the reality of life in the universe. There is no one on Earth that can teach you about the Greater Community, for how would they know?

Only a New Message from the Creator of all life can reveal these things to you, things that have never been revealed to humanity before, but which humanity now needs to prepare for its encounter with life beyond its borders and to give you the strength and the vision to face and navigate the Great Waves of change that are coming to the world.

I speak from beyond your visible range because I speak for Creation. All of Us have lived in this world and other worlds before, as have many of you.

Your theologies are far too narrow and limited to encompass the meaning of your spirituality and the scope of time that it truly encompasses. But everyone must have a starting point. And everyone must have the beneficence of the Creator, and so many different pathways to God have been provided. And they have all been altered and changed by people over time.

It is now time for you to learn the theology of the Greater Community. If you do not learn this, you will never evolve beyond being a primitive race, isolated and ignorant, superstitious and foolish in your comprehension of life. That is why there is a New Revelation in the world, you see. And that is why it is unlike anything that humanity has ever received before.

People will not understand it. People will be confused. Some people will be outraged and threatened. But God's Revelation is not given to meet people's expectations.

It is given to save humanity. Humanity could perish in the face of the Great Waves of change. Humanity could perish in its encounter with the Greater Community of intelligent life, a Greater Community that is not human and which does not value the human spirit.

That is why there is a New Revelation. That is why your comprehension now must be greater. You must begin to think of things that you have never thought of before, to break down the distinctions you have made that have no place in a real understanding and to make new distinctions that must be made in order for the new understanding to emerge. It will take a long time for people to learn this, but even if a few can, it is a beginning.

There are many in the world today who are feeling the Spirit stirring within themselves, preparing for a new reality and a New Revelation. They have not found their home in the traditions of the world. They are waiting for something new to be revealed. They are living in the future because their present life cannot account for their deeper yearning or their greater associations. If they can discover the New Revelation, it will bring clarity and meaning to their existence and will answer their questions—questions that they could only live with otherwise, with no possible answer in sight.

It is important for you now to know that you have come into the world at this time and that each of you has been given a greater purpose—to serve the world as it exists and to serve the world into the future so that humanity may have a future, and the evolution of the human family may continue with a greater possibility for success.

It is time to outgrow creation stories and the end of the world ideas, for reality exists so far beyond these things. It is time now to look to the heavens, to contemplate the great expanse of the universe and to reconsider your fundamental beliefs and ideas, if they have been formulated at all.

Human spirituality has been limited to this world and to local regions within this world, and to the history of those regions and those races and those peoples. But Greater Community Spirituality is a spirituality of the entire universe. God is the God of the entire universe—a God of countless races quite unlike you, a universe that represents practical, physical and spiritual evolution in every conceivable stage. That is what you will be facing in the future. And that is why you cannot be a primitive people with primitive ideas. You too must grow and expand because life is requiring this of you now.

The Revelations must come and they must be great, great enough to serve humanity for a very long time. Here is where all the great traditions of the world find a greater panorama of expression. Here is where the unity of their intention can become recognized, and all the differences between them—the differences in understanding, the differences in spiritual practice and emphasis and the differences in their teachers, their leaders and their Messengers—begin to fall away to reveal their greater presence and intention.

The purpose of all religion is to bring you to Knowledge. For Knowledge is here to guide you, to protect you and to lead you to a greater life in service to the world. Be you of any faith or tradition, this is the case.

You may pray to God. You may fall down on your knees and prostrate yourself in the temple or the mosque or the church. But until you begin to carry out God's Work that is meant for you to carry out, you will not understand the real nature of your spiritual reality.

These things exist, but they must be relearned, for the Separation is blinding and confusing and overwhelming in its manifestation. It too is a reality that seems perpetual even though it does have an end. But the end time for the universe is so far beyond your concept of time that for you it has no end. Within the scope of your life, it has no end.

Therefore, accept this teaching and the preparation to allow your mind to outgrow its shackles, its constraints and its delusions so that it may serve the power of Knowledge within you and not be an impediment to Knowledge.

For your mind is a vehicle of communication. It is not your true Self and nature. The intellect is a powerful communicator and a powerful navigator. It is here to guide your ship. But you must be the captain of this ship, and this is where the preparation must begin. This is where you must look and see that which limits you and that which expands your life, that which leads you to the power and the presence of Knowledge and that which denies this presence and takes you away from it.

You have no origin, so the soul cannot die. But if the soul is living in a hellish state, then its suffering seems to have no end. It is a prisoner in the reality of Separation. This Separation has an end. But it is an end far beyond the scope of this life, an end that you will work for in different capacities even as you outgrow the need to live in this world or to even take form.

That is why the notions of Heaven and Hell are primitive notions and have no bearing on reality. Should you succeed in outgrowing the need to take form, then you will be of service to those who remain behind. Thus, your service will grow. God will not waste your accomplishments, but put them to use to serve others who need them and who will rely upon them in the future.

Here everything that is religious must be reconsidered in the Light of the New Revelation. Here you must realize that you are not your intellect and that the intellect alone cannot grasp the nature of God's Presence and Intention in the world. That can only come through Revelation, the Revelation given to the whole world and the revelation that must occur within your life as an individual, that brings you to the power and the presence of Knowledge and shows you the limits of your thinking and understanding.

This is a gift to liberate you, to strengthen you and to give you the power of purpose in the world. But there is so much in the way, so many deeply held beliefs and assumptions. People have built their whole career on beliefs and assumptions. People base their identity on beliefs and assumptions.

These doors must be opened and re-examined. This requires courage and fortitude. For humanity is not ready for the Great Waves of change, for living in a world in decline—a world of diminishing resources, a world of environmental constraints. Humanity is not prepared for the realities of life in the universe, which are far more challenging than you can now imagine. That is why a New Revelation has to be given now, and why humanity's understanding must grow. Human unity and cooperation must be built and established, not out of high principle, but really for survival and creation.

You will see in the future who is wise and who is not, who can respond to Revelation and who cannot, whose heart is open and whose is not, who has the courage to challenge their own ideas and the ideas of their societies and who does not. In the Light of Revelation, all this will become revealed, for no one can live in the past when the future is being revealed.

The Creator of all life loves the human spirit and all the peoples in the world, whether they have a religion or not, whether they are wise or foolish, whether they are sinful or virtuous. It just changes the amount of work that must be done to redeem them, in time. But to God, time is nothing. To you, time is everything, as it should be, as it is.

Your destiny is in the Greater Community. Your isolation is over. You are exhausting the world's resources. To be free in the universe, you must be self-sufficient, you must be united and you must be very discreet. These are the requirements for all free races in the universe. But this will require a great change in human understanding and human behavior, and a great liberation from your past and the limits of your past beliefs.

People do not change very willingly, so this will take time. But time is what you do not have a great deal of to prepare. That is why there is a New Revelation in the world. That is why there is a preparation for humanity. Not everyone has to prepare. But enough have to prepare in all nations and faith traditions for humanity to begin to gain a real comprehension of its predicament and its great opportunities.

There is nothing more important in the world than this, for everything that is valuable can be lost in the face of the great challenges to come. That is why there is nothing more important for you as an individual and for the human family to receive than the New Revelation.

With Knowledge, you will know how to proceed. Without Knowledge, you will enter increasing frustration, confusion and despair in the face of the great trials and uncertainty that are coming. This is God's Prophecy for humanity. God's Messenger is here to provide this.

There are thousands of spiritual teachings in the world today, but there is only one Messenger. There is only one New Message from God. If you do not accept this, it is because you are afraid that the answer has finally been given and that it will require great things of you and a greater responsibility for you.

You will see who can respond and who cannot, and all the reasons that people give for denying that which has the promise to save the human family. The light exposes the darkness and all that is hidden there. The light reveals that which was hidden, that which was concealed, that which was falsely called by other names. In this time of Revelation, you will see that which is true and that which is false. And the distinctions will be clear.

Have great faith, then, that the power and the presence of Knowledge are with you. It remains uncorrupted within you. Your mind is confused, afraid and full of limiting and false ideas. But the power of Knowledge is with you. That is why your life has great promise despite your circumstances and the difficulties of the day.

The preparation is demanding, for freedom must be won. It cannot merely be assumed. You must give up that which denies it for it to become strong within you. It is a demand upon men. It is a requirement, and not merely a consolation.

Hear, then, the Voice that speaks for the Power of Creation—a Voice greater than your own, a Voice beyond an individual, a Voice that speaks for a great Presence and Hierarchy in the world, a Voice you cannot identify, a Voice that is not part of your traditions. But it is this Voice that spoke to the great emancipators and Messengers in the past, a Voice like this, taking them beyond their current understanding and preparing them to provide this to their peoples to the best of their abilities.

Respond to this great calling and your life will begin to move, and your errors will become apparent. It will begin to change your allegiance to people, places and things as an act that is natural and fundamental and in harmony with your deeper experience.

God only asks that you return to what is true within yourself and within other people. You do not have to be magnificent or absolutely pure or flawless, for that will not occur. Even the greatest amongst you will have doubts and inhibitions.

Let this be your understanding.

CHAPTER 4

THE SEPARATION

As revealed to
Marshall Vian Summers
on November 25, 2012
in Boulder, Colorado

To understand the reality of God and God's Work in the world and in the universe around you, you must understand your own situation clearly, for you are living in a state of Separation, in a physical reality, in time and space. Your life here is limited by this time and this space.

You are functioning like a creature on the Earth, but you are greater than this by far. Your deeper nature is connected to where you have come from and to what you will return to beyond this life and world.

You are living in Separation from your Source and from Creation itself, which exist beyond the physical reality entirely. You are living in a temporary reality. It is impermanent. It is changing. It is expanding. It is chaotic. It is governed by its own laws and dynamics.

You are a spiritual Being living in a physical reality. This accounts for your dual nature and the fundamental conflict and confusion that permeate your mind and activities. It is the result of Separation fundamentally.

You cannot yet be who you really are in this world and life without undergoing a great preparation, which the Lord of all the universes has provided for you in a new and revolutionary form, free of human intervention, manipulation and corruption.

Likewise, you cannot simply be a creature on the Earth, for this denies your deeper reality and your greater intelligence. Though many people have made this assumption, they cannot deny the fact that there is a greater power in their life and a greater dimension to their own personal reality.

To be a sentient being living in a physical universe means you must have a deeper conscience and a deeper reality, or you will be miserable at all counts—limited, overwhelmed, endangered, constantly facing problem solving and dilemmas, many of which you cannot resolve. Life becomes hellish despite its beautiful appearances and its simple pleasures.

To become really true to yourself and right with yourself, you must gain access to your deeper nature, which is still connected to Creation and still connected to that Greater Reality from which you have come and to which you will return.

This goes far beyond people's notions of Heaven and Hell, far beyond ancient teachings constructed for primitive peoples, far beyond what humanity can understand intellectually at this point. For you are not only separated from Creation, you are separated from your Source, and you are separated from your deeper nature. For all three are associated, you see, and are part of the same reality.

People may well ask, "Well, why Separation?" Creation is free. If you choose not to be a part of it, you are free to leave. But you would have nowhere to leave if God had not established the physical universe as a place for the separated to live. This alternative reality, which seems to be your complete reality from where you see at this moment, is but a very small part of Creation. That is how big Creation really is.

Beyond the stars, beyond the galaxies, there is Creation. And Creation is not merely what is beyond. It is what is here at this moment. You are living in Creation right now though your eyes cannot see it. Your hands cannot touch it. Your ears cannot hear it. For these faculties of mind and body have not been developed sufficiently to discern this greater reality in which you live every moment of every day.

So it is not like you left there and came here. You simply shifted into a different dimension from where you were to begin with. That is why those who sent you into this reality are still with you now. It is not like they are far away and you are far from home. It is very confusing to the intellect, which can only deal with one dimension at a time to even consider this. But it is true nonetheless.

Accept the limits of your intellect. It was never designed to answer the greater questions of life or to understand your deeper nature or purpose in the world. It is a wonderful mechanism, a great servant to Spirit. This is its true function and value.

But Creation and even the physical universe expand so far beyond your boundaries, your capacity intellectually, that you are unwise to attempt to go there, for you will only find confusion, frustration and the pain of finding your own limits, which you can never exceed intellectually.

Why the Separation? The real answer to this is why you want to be separate in this moment, why you do not want to hear the greater voice that God has put within you—the voice of Knowledge, the voice that resonates through your deeper nature, which is still connected to God. Why do you reject this? Why do you avoid this? Why do you want to live out in the world and be lost there, consumed by your interests, your hobbies and your dilemmas? Why do you run away from that which will redeem you?

The question [Why the Separation?] is important, but ultimately the answer must be found within your own experience, beneath the surface of your mind. Stay at the surface of your mind, acting and reacting to the world, and you will never understand any of these things even though they hold the ultimate value and purpose of your life and the meaning of your existence in this world, at this time, under these circumstances, no matter how troubling they may seem.

In Creation, you are free. You are so free, you are even free not to be in Creation. But since there is nowhere for you to go in Creation to not be in Creation, God created an alternative reality and gave it an evolutionary track—a beginning, an expanding universe. And it has been populated by all those who have sought this experience, for whatever reason.

But because you cannot be separate from yourself for very long, your life in this alternative reality would be temporary. And because the only way you cannot be who you really are is to be distracted and obsessed by your surroundings, this temporary reality would be problematic. It would be difficult. It would be dangerous. It would be changing. It would be unpredictable. It would be confusing.

For if this alternative reality were as quiescent and beautiful as your Ancient Home, you would simply reawaken immediately, and your desire for Separation would end very quickly. So in order for you to maintain this state, this desire to be unique and separate, to enter into this other reality, it must be very challenging, you see. Otherwise, you would lose interest in it right away. It would not captivate you, and you want to be captivated if you seek Separation.

The real mystery of this is still embedded in your experience, in the decisions you make every day: whether to judge and condemn and thus deepen your Separation; whether to run away from your deeper experience, which could bring you closer to your deeper nature; whether you avoid and deny those experiences, difficulties and opportunities that could call this greater power of Knowledge out of you; why you become obsessed with people, places and things; why you are so easily distracted; why you live in confusion and debate, trying to define life with simple statements.

Even your religious affiliation is shallow and has very little depth in it. If you are still seeking Separation, you do not want to go very far or very deep with anyone or anything, for this would bring you back to yourself. This would bring you back to Knowledge within you, which God has put there now to guide you and bless you in this difficult alternative reality.

People ask, "Well, are human beings simply part of the evolutionary process of life on Earth? Did human beings originate from simple life forms?" Well, no. For a sentient being to enter into this reality, they must have a physical vehicle that is capable of expressing their intentions and their creativity. Otherwise, it would simply be a prison house and would be intolerable. So sentient beings have to wait a long time for the evolutionary process to create such a vehicle for them to inhabit, a body capable of doing marvelous things—of altering the landscape, for better or worse; for changing reality; for adapting to reality; for building structures; for building towns and villages and cities and nations eventually—to create greater and greater stability and security for those living in this difficult physical reality.

Imagine if you were a sentient being, but you were only given the body of a dog or a bird. You could not change anything; you could not fix anything; you could not alter anything. You would be stranded in this very restrained and difficult life by your physical vehicle itself.

God wants you to learn and create in this world and to contribute to its well-being and the value of others, which you could not do if you did not have a marvelous instrument, a marvelous vehicle, a marvelous body in which to function. You could not communicate without this. You could not express yourself. You could not create anything. God loves you even if you seek Separation, so God assures that your experience of Separation can ultimately be meaningful for you.

Think of what We are saying in light of the creation stories that have been invented through religious traditions. Symbolic though they may be, they are utterly ridiculous in terms of reality. Reality is so much greater than human estimation.

It is understandable that people would try to create simple stories in a childlike state of mind. But the universe is full of a billion, billion, billion races and more, and they have all sought Separation from Creation in this reality. And they are very different from each other, having followed different evolutionary tracks in different environments, interacting with each other, for better or worse— civilizations rising, civilizations falling.

Your God is their God too, you see. That is why your strict definitions of divinity are so limited and have to be considered to be very, very unique to you and your thoughts. But they cannot encompass reality. They are relative by the very nature of your life in this world. For there is nothing absolute here except the Power and the Presence of God and what God has given within you to follow—to guide you, to protect you and to lead you to your greater fulfillment in this difficult and changing reality.

THE SEPARATION

People may ask, "Well, why should I care about Separation and what you are saying here?" We say it is because it has everything to do with who you are and why you are in the world and why you suffer and why you have limitations and why you need the greater strength and power that God has put within you to guide you, to protect you and to lead you to a greater life. It has everything to do with your unique design as an individual, which was made for you to assume a specific role in the world, something you could not understand unless this role became apparent to you and you were able to recognize it, receive it and prepare for it.

Otherwise, having intelligence in life is a curse—aware of your death, fearful of all that you might lose, living in anxiety and apprehension, seeing the dangers of the world around you, ever fearful, ever guarded, ever resentful, ever angry, ever feeling weak and helpless.

The animals are happier than you because they do not think these things. They are unaware of these things. They can live in the moment even though they might die in the next hour. They are living in the moment. They do not see or know their end until the moment it occurs. They do not see it. They do not worry about it. It is not a concern. They are trying to live and get what they need every day.

For a sentient being, though, the awareness of the future and the regrets from the past are an immense burden and source of suffering and misery. Only a greater purpose in life can utilize the past and the future for a greater purpose, thus relieving you from the suffering and the anxiety that they would otherwise produce in an overwhelming way.

Without this greater purpose, people are sedated. They are obsessed. They are addicted to drugs. They are addicted to people. They are fixated because they are trying to escape their own misery, their own anxiety, their own uncertainty, their own grievances, their own fear in all of its manifestations.

Do not condemn people for being obsessed and fixated. They are trying to escape something you are trying to escape. They are just taking the wrong path, that is all. Their approach is futile and dangerous and self-destructive.

God has given you the antidote to living in the physical reality. The antidote is the deeper Knowledge God has placed within you. Beyond the realm and the reach of the intellect it is. You cannot understand it with your intellect. You can only respond to it and follow it and allow it to demonstrate to you its power and efficacy.

For Knowledge within you is without fear. It is not corrupted by the world. It represents the eternal part of you that is going to live beyond this world. But it is concerned that you may fulfill your destiny here, and to that end it works ceaselessly on your behalf, trying to orient you through many different means to follow a true direction, to stick with that direction and not to lose heart or be pulled off track by beauty, wealth and charm or by despair and anguish.

So while God allowed the universe to be created, the physical universe you live in, God also gave the antidote to suffering and to Separation at the very beginning because you cannot really be separate from your Creator and from Creation. Even being obsessed in the physical reality, you still cannot escape your origin and your greater destiny.

It is then all a matter of time, and time here can be equated with suffering, the suffering you experience to various degrees every day of your life. You do not even know how much you are suffering because you do not know what it is like to be free of it, except perhaps for brief moments here and there. Even your state you call "normal" is a state of suffering—a state of apprehension, concern and anxiety; a state overshadowed by the difficulties of life and the great change that is happening in the world at this time.

It is hard for people to be honest about this. They are so adapted to their own misery that they call things "good" that are not good. They accept things that are unacceptable. They adapt to situations that are harmful or unfulfilling for them. Even if they live in a free nation and can alter their circumstances, they will cling to things that have no promise or benefit for them. For security, for approval, they will stay in a situation that can never really benefit them.

They will lose their inspiration and will become jaded. They will give up hope and believe in miracles, and believe in Heaven, and believe in a great saint or prophet, for they really cannot receive what God has given to them, which lives within them at this moment.

It is a tragic situation. Separation is tragic. It is the source of all suffering and confusion, anxiety and self-condemnation. It is a terrible thing, really, but it is understandable. It is the outcome of living in Separation. For you can never be fully happy or satisfied living in a world like this, no matter how beautiful or interesting it really is.

And if you were to be immortal in this environment, you would soon find out that you would tire of it. You would tire of its constant problem solving, its constant dilemmas, its constant stress and its constant change. You would tire of it and seek a greater reality and involvement. That is why your life is temporary, you see. Otherwise, it would become ever more hellish for you.

As it is, your prison house can be escaped. If you were to be immortal here, there would be no escape. You would be stranded in a reality that does not represent your Ancient Home, your greater purpose, your deeper nature or the true meaning of your existence. Here you are just a creature with a name, a feature on the landscape, utterly dispensable as far as nature is concerned.

That is why you must turn to your deeper nature. For God does not want to bring you out of the world. God does not reclaim you through death. God wants you to live a real life here so that your Ancient Home can be brought into this place of Separation, so that you may bring your gifts and the spirit of giving here that represent a Greater Reality that everyone needs and that everyone is looking for in various ways.

God redeems you through the power and presence of Knowledge within you. Knowledge will prepare you to become a contributor to life so that your real unique gifts can be given where they are needed and the power of this giving may redeem you and replace the regrets, the hatred and the self-condemnation that still abide with you each day.

God is with you even in your state of Separation, both as a Presence and as a living reality deep within you. For you cannot escape your Source, and that is why ultimately your redemption is guaranteed. Even the deepest depths of Hell will be emptied eventually, for you can never leave Creation permanently. You can only leave it temporarily, and this is a great blessing, you see.

You may cling to life. You may be attached to the people, places and things of life, but your Spirit would become restless here if your work is complete. That does not mean to say that everyone dies when they are ready or when they should, for many people perish quite unnecessarily through conflict, war, disease and deprivation. That is part of the tragedy of the human condition in this world, a condition that is shared throughout the universe, the Greater Community of life in which you have always lived.

So you are separate from God in your own mind. You are separate from Creation because you are living in an alternative reality that does not represent Creation entirely. And you are separate from your deeper nature, which is still connected to God and represents the eternal part of you.

God has put a Greater Intelligence within you now to guide and bless you as you are living in this difficult and challenging reality. The purpose of all religion is to bring you to this Knowledge and to engage you with your deeper nature.

You are not here to please God. You are not here to earn merits. You are not here to escape Hell. You are here to contribute because that is what will redeem you. That is how Hell will be escaped. That is how you will resonate with your Source and Creator.

No matter what your religious tradition, or if you have no religious tradition, it is the same, you see. But the purpose of religion has been altered. It has become about hero worship and adherence to ideas and beliefs. It has degenerated, you see, over time. It has lost its primary focus and function. These can still be found in the great traditions, but you would need a wise and very clear teacher as a guide to find them, for they are overlaid with the ornamentation, the ritual and the human commentary associated with religion.

It is like the treasure is in the temple, but it is locked deep inside, and you have to go find it. That, in part, is why God has sent a New Revelation into the world, to provide the Steps to Knowledge in the clearest possible form that can be translated into any language and studied directly, powerfully, without human commentary and without the weight and the corruption of history oppressing it.

An answer to the Separation was given the moment it began. That answer lives within you today. You have a greater destiny in the world, and you have a greater destiny beyond the world, no matter who you are—even if you are living in a different world, even if you are not a human being.

God's Plan is for everyone in the entire universe. That is why your notions about redemption have been so limited before this. For what God is doing in the universe is what God is doing in your world. And until the great Revelation of your time, which is happening now, how would you ever know what God is doing in the universe?

You can see how easy it is to be confused about these matters and how human beings have crafted religion to meet their needs, their fears and their anxieties. Yet the blessing is upon you because Knowledge lives within you.

Do not try to call the physical universe the same as your Heavenly state, for they are very, very different. Do not think your mind and your body and your Spirit are all going to live forever, for only one is permanent. The others are temporary.

Do not think that belief is going to get you into Heaven, for when you leave this world, you will not have any beliefs. You will just be who you are. And your life will not be evaluated based on your beliefs, but on the degree of service you were able to give to a world in need, and the degree to which you were able to forgive others and to be compassionate.

THE SEPARATION

There is no special dispensation if you are a Christian, a Muslim or a Buddhist. God does not care what religion you belong to as long as it can bring you to the deeper Knowledge that God has placed within you. That is the Ancient Covenant you have with God, you see. Religion can be very helpful if it is understood correctly, but God's Power and God's Redemption exist even beyond the reaches of religion.

This is the universal spirituality. You are living in a Greater Community of life. You are emerging into this Greater Community. That is part of the great threshold that humanity is facing at this time. That is why you must learn about spirituality in the Greater Community and begin to understand the real nature of Creation, the origin and the destiny of the universe you see and sense and the reality of your purpose and meaning in this world—what brought you here and what can fulfill you here, given the power and presence of Knowledge within you.

Your redemption is [assured] because you can never be separate from God entirely. This is what will save you in the end, but the end can be far into the future. It is your decision about whether to receive the blessing, the power and the grace that God has placed within you and allow this to redirect your life, to give it coherence, meaning and real value, and to bring into your life great relationships and to re-establish great relationships that already exist.

Before you can give these greater things, you must receive and take the Steps to Knowledge. Ultimately, you will understand why Separation occurred as you unravel Separation within yourself, as you take the Steps to Knowledge and as you reunite your worldly mind with the deeper mind of Knowledge within you. This will begin to end the Separation within yourself, which will completely alter your experience of being in the world—your sense of destiny, strength, power and purpose in this temporary place.

Let this be your understanding.

CHAPTER 5

WHAT IS CREATION?

As revealed to
Marshall Vian Summers
on February 4, 2008
in Boulder, Colorado

It is time now for humanity to learn of spirituality in the Greater Community of life in which your world has always existed. It is time now to outgrow tribal focus and tribal identification to learn a new paradigm, to realize the evolution of religious understanding in the universe where it has been most fully expressed and where it has been most greatly achieved.

Humanity now must gain a greater perspective in order to establish human unity and understanding, to meet and to face the Great Waves of change that are coming to the world and to recognize and to offset the Greater Darkness that is in the world.

You cannot meet a new reality with an old understanding, and that is why God has sent a New Message into the world, a Message for the protection and advancement of humanity.

The first question is: What is Creation? Creation is all that God has created within time and beyond time. You live within time, so you live in a part of Creation that is in motion, that is in flux, that is unstable and that is evolving and expanding. This part of Creation was established to provide a home for the separated, where they could experience Separation and have the opportunity to choose a way to return to that part of Creation that does not change, that is complete and eternal.

The Creation that you must be concerned with is this temporary Creation—a place of time and space, a physical reality, a reality of constant change, of evolving systems, a reality of contrast and conflict, a reality of life and death.

Separation created this reality, for God knew that the separated must have a foundation upon which to exist. This has set in train the physical universe that you are only beginning to comprehend and that you must learn to serve and to recognize if you are to outgrow its fascinations and to forgive its tragedies.

Creation beyond this is beyond your awareness now, though you are actually living within it. For the temporary Creation is happening at another level. You are already surrounded by the permanent Creation, but your eyes cannot see it, your ears cannot hear it and your fingers cannot touch it because your senses were only established to recognize physical things and things that are moving, objects that are moving and sounds that are changing.

The greater reality in which you live is all around you. You have never left it, but given your reliance upon your senses, you cannot experience it directly without a certain kind of preparation.

This is entirely confounding to your human understanding, and this is entirely confounding to the understanding of the countless races of beings who live within the Greater Community of intelligent life that comprises the physical universe in which you live. They are all living in Separation. They are all experiencing evolution. They represent the evolution of consciousness, technology and social establishment at every conceivable level.

This is all happening within the permanent Creation itself. For while there appears to be Separation and you live in this separated state— where everything seems to be distinct and unique; where everything is changing and moving, being born and dying—you have not left the permanent Creation. It is still here.

The Separation is fundamentally a problem in perception, communication and awareness. There have been very few individuals in the history of humanity who have been able to break through the veil that seems to separate this physical, temporary, changing reality from your permanent reality that represents your Ancient Home— where God is known, where you are known, where there are no questions for there are no conflicts, where change does not exist for it is not needed.

This is inconceivable to you in your current state, and it is not even desirable given your priorities and objectives. But it is important for you to know that the Separation has not really succeeded and that the break from God has not really been accomplished. It is real in your current experience of reality, within this partial Creation in which you exist. But it is separated. That is why it is changing and that is why it is evolving.

If life in the physical were not changing and evolving, it would be Hell for you. Imagine being in a reality that you did not like, a reality that never changed. You would have no hope. You would make no progress. And even if that physical reality, that unchanging physical reality, were perfect in meeting all your perceived needs, after a while you would see that living in a body is inherently uncomfortable, problematic and difficult, and you would want to be free. But you could not be free, in that case, for you would have established a kind of [immortality] in your imagined physical reality, and you would be trapped, you see.

Hell is a beautiful place where you can never be happy. That is Hell. If you were in a place of real torment, you would want to go home to God right away. But here, in this beautiful Hell, you are ambivalent; you are attached. It intrigues you; it seduces you; it mesmerizes you. And though you fear its dangers, its terrors and its unpredictability in this current physical reality, you are still fixated upon it.

So for you, Creation is the physical universe. It seems to be forever, but it is really temporary. It has a beginning, a middle and an end. You have not even reached the middle spot of this expanding universe, so this is something that is confounding to your understanding.

It is important for you to know, should you ever think that immortality in the physical realm is desirable, you must recognize that such a state would be Hell itself. To be in a beautiful place where you could never be happy would be extremely hellish and you would be held there for a long time because you would keep wanting it, believing in it, hoping for it and trying to make it work.

The fact that your physical reality is constantly changing, expanding and evolving and is going through growth and decay gives you hope and promise that your greater purpose and the need of the soul may be fulfilled here.

This requires an entirely different theological and philosophical foundation. If you believe you are in the world because you have sinned or because you have been condemned, then you will not recognize the great opportunity that exists within your reality for your redemption. Indeed, given the philosophical foundations of many of the world's religions today, it makes this picture incredibly complex, unclear and difficult to discern.

Yet God has placed Knowledge within you, a deeper mind, a deeper understanding. And this Knowledge holds your purpose and direction and the promise of your greater accomplishments in the world.

Because you have entered Separation, you must now serve the Separation. You must serve people and life existing in this separated state. This is how you rediscover and re-experience the permanence of your Ancient Home.

Redemption is not simply pleasing God and going to Heaven or not pleasing God and going to Hell. This is ridiculous. This represents a purely human separated state of mind and perception. You believe that the righteous should be rewarded and the wicked should be punished and that God will give the rewards and do the punishment. You imagine God to be like yourself—to have your temperament, to have your values, to uphold your sense of justice and to meet your criteria and expectations. This is foolish and arrogant, of course, but this is the position of many people.

But do not worry, for everyone in the physical universe, the countless races of beings in all stages of evolution, has the same kinds of assumptions. It is to be expected. God is not fooled by it. God is not upset by it. It is simply the result of living in a separated state.

Even your notions of religion and spirituality are founded within this separated state. People imagine Heaven to be kind of a perfect version of their physical reality without realizing that should such a reality ever be created, it would be Hell itself. To be in a beautiful place where you could never be happy would be a kind of ongoing Hell.

God cannot make you happy by the stroke of a wand or by some spell. You must return to your permanent state as God created you, not as a conflicted individual. You would not be able to even experience your permanent reality as a conflicted, unhappy individual. You would see the projections of your own mind. You would want to be in an environment that represented your own conflicted state, and that is what keeps you here.

You could be in a worse state. You could experience Hell more thoroughly. You could be more miserable, certainly. There seems to be no end to the degrees of misery that people are willing to accommodate and to adapt themselves to.

But nonetheless, Creation is complete, and your temporary experience in this temporary reality that you call the physical universe is but a tiny part of God's permanent Creation—a Creation that you cannot yet experience clearly for yourself, even though you might have glimpses here and there.

People's beliefs and assumptions, their metaphysical ideas, their religious values and their speculations all suffer from a kind of level confusion. They try to imagine a permanent blessed state called Heaven, but they cannot see it as it really is. They cannot resonate with it yet as it really is, for they are not ready for that. They have not yet been prepared for Heaven, to return. They are not complete in their service here in the physical reality. They have not completed their mission here.

When the Separation began, before any of your estimations of time or history, the solution was instantly created. For while the Separation may fool you, may captivate you, may mesmerize you, may trap you and all other entities and beings who are in the physical reality at this time, it did not fool God. It may be foolproof, but it is not Godproof.

So the solution was created immediately. But in time, it seems to take such a great deal of experience for the solution to be accepted, experienced and expressed.

You are lingering in time. Time is the interval between the point at which you left your permanent Creation to the time in which you finally return to it completely. That interval is called time. Time is inconceivable and unnecessary in your permanent reality because time is related to change. It is related to events that change. It is something that marks the progression of events.

The whole notion of time is part of the adaptation to living within a physical reality. It is a form of measurement that was established out of necessity to be able to organize one's thoughts and actions, to be able to interface with a changing physical reality, to be able to mark one's progress and accomplishments, and to understand one's history and past and the history and the past of others who have dwelt here. Time is unnecessary in your permanent reality. It is irrelevant.

You can see from Our words here how far you are from yet being able to experience this or resonate with it. Perhaps it intrigues you. Perhaps it stirs an ancient memory in you. Perhaps there are aspects of it that you yearn for. Perhaps it looks boring to you and unexciting and unappealing to be living in a changeless reality.

You are so addicted to change. You love change and you hate change. You love your physical existence and you hate your physical existence. It intrigues you. It stimulates you. And yet it hurts you, terrifies you and disappoints you.

It is this seemingly irreconcilable problem, confusion and dichotomy that God's answer addresses directly. For God has placed within you a deeper intelligence that is not confused by what confuses your thinking, worldly mind. It is not befuddled by the world. It is not deceived by appearances. It is not attracted to all the things that seem to induce you, seduce you and allure you. It is not terrified by what terrifies you. It is not afraid of change, loss and death. For it is the permanent part of you. It is the part of you that could never separate from God.

This Knowledge is within you now. It is here on a mission to contribute within certain circumstances, with certain individuals, to achieve certain things. Its ultimate purpose is beyond your comprehension, but the steps that it provides for you are immediately accessible and can be discerned if you are willing, open and capable. It resolves the dilemma because it expresses the reality of your Ancient Home through you while you are here in this temporary physical reality. It demonstrates a greater power, a greater resonance and a greater relationship. And it provides real, tangible service here in the world where people are suffering. They are languishing in time. They are experiencing desperation and hopelessness. And the world is facing great travail in the near future.

God is not careless in this matter. God sends into the world what is needed to keep everyone here moving in a positive direction. People in this reality have the decision and the power to make the world more a reflection of their Ancient Home or a more hellish place.

CHAPTER 6

THE SOUL

As revealed to
Marshall Vian Summers
on November 2, 2009
in Boulder, Colorado

Any consideration of the soul must only be relative to your current circumstances, stage of development and the range of reality that you are able to experience. This, of course, is the challenge facing any idea of spiritual truth in the world—that it is all relative to where you are looking from and your position in the universe and in Creation.

Therefore, what may be true within this reality may not hold true in the next dimension of reality that you will experience most certainly when you leave this world. Fighting and arguing and going to war over religious ideas is a fool's errand, at the very least, and an utter tragedy in reality.

To think that the scriptures alone can tell you the Mind and the Will of God is a great underestimation. For you must experience this at the level of Knowledge within yourself.

Religion is a pathway to an intellectual dead end, or it is a pathway to the discovery of the soul, and the great need of the soul to fulfill its mission and destiny in the world, in service to humanity and in service to the world. Everyone was sent into the world to serve the world. But, of course, this initial and fundamental intention has been lost and confused, twisted and corrupted, leading to the world you experience today.

So the question arises: What is the soul? We shall give you an understanding here that will be very helpful, as long as you remember that this understanding, and any understanding We give you of things dealing with the eternal, will grow and change as you progress. What you tell a child about the world is not what you tell an adult. What you tell a child about God is not what you tell an adult. Therefore, the degree of your maturity will really determine your awareness and your understanding, particularly dealing with realities that extend beyond this world and beyond this brief period of life that you call life in the world.

The soul's reality certainly fits into this category. It was created before you came into the world, and it will exist after you leave the world. So your worldly understanding, which is extremely temporary given the limits of your time and activity in the world, will only give you a glimpse of it from a certain perspective.

But clarity here is always important to allow your mind to expand and to remind you that who you are is not your intellect, or the range of your ideas, or your memories, or your grievances and so forth. What has been created in the world will pass with the world in your experience to a very large degree.

What is the soul? The soul is the part of you that God created that is permanent and that existed before this life and will continue beyond this life.

The question then arises: What is Knowledge that you speak of? Knowledge is the part of your soul that has not separated from God, and thus is able to respond to the Will of God, to the protection of God and to the Wisdom of God as it pertains to your particular life and circumstances, in this situation of living in the world.

So, in essence, your soul and Knowledge are not yet the same in your experience. Your soul in your experience, living in a state of Separation, is the part of your permanent identity that has separated from God. But since you cannot completely separate from God, the part of you that did not separate from God represents your saving grace.

Reunite the soul with Knowledge and the soul is complete, and Separation within the soul has been ended. In other words, part of the soul is journeying through life as a separate entity, unaware and afraid of confronting its true reality. The part of the soul that has never left God goes along, but it is responding to something very different and is a very different kind of intelligence.

The Separation was never complete because you cannot separate yourself from your Source. Even though you may attempt to do this and invest yourself greatly in this effort, in the end, it cannot be successful. That is why all souls, eventually in time, perhaps in the very great distant future, will reunite with God.

The moment that Separation was created, before the creation of time and space, the answer was given. The answer was given because you could not separate from God, and that is what will save you in the end. No matter what your religious affiliation or system of belief, no matter what your time, your culture—even no matter what world you exist in in the Greater Community of worlds in the universe—this is your salvation.

You return to God through Knowledge, Knowledge being the greater part of you that has never separated from God. We use the term Knowledge because it is related to the ability to have profound experiences of recognition and knowing. Here Knowledge is not a body of information or what you learn at the university. Here

Knowledge is not a system of belief or a philosophy or a theology. It is the movement of Spirit within you.

So what We are saying here is that your Spirit is divided. That is where the Separation happened, you see. It is not like you got kicked out of Heaven or you went off in a huff, angry with God: "I'm going to create my own reality!" Like a lovers' quarrel: "I'm going to go off on my own! I don't need you! I'm going to go live without you. I'm going to go be in isolation," as a kind of spiteful activity, you see.

Of course, you go into isolation, and you suffer. Disconnected from your Source, you now have no security. You have no sense of permanence. You have no sense of intrinsic relationship. You take refuge in the world as an individual. You adopt form. You develop an intellect to navigate the world because it is such a difficult and unpredictable place. And from this position of isolation, separation and embodiment, you try to understand what God is.

God has sent Messages periodically into the world at great turning points for humanity. These Revelations have been captured by the minds and the imaginations, altered and applied, and distorted to the point where they are full of truth and ignorance. To find your way within them, which you can certainly do, you must separate the truth from the ignorance.

You cannot know God with your intellect. It was not created to encompass something so great. For an intellect can only consider other intellects. It can only consider things that are like itself to some degree, and God is not an intellect. People think of God as a person or a personage, but God is not a person or a personage.

Extending ever beyond your grasp and concepts and attempt to formulate and to limit God, God exists. It would be like an ant trying to understand the sun of your solar system. It can experience the power of the sun, and benefits from this to be able to live in the world that you know, but comprehension will never really be complete.

The Revelations from God have always been for the purpose of re-engaging you with your deeper nature so that the Separation can be mended and finally ended within you. For you cannot return to your Ancient Home, your heavenly state, until this mending has occurred. God cannot un-create your Separation because God did not create the Separation.

God affects reality, not that which is not reality. But God has sent Knowledge with you into the world. It goes everywhere with you. In this way, God does not have to take care of your life and does not have to watch over you personally because the Lord of a trillion universes cannot be preoccupied with your daily affairs, or your preoccupations or internal conflicts. To think that God is talking to you every day is to make God into your personal servant, your errand boy, like some kind of minor deity that is preoccupied with what you are doing.

God is the Great Attraction calling you back, calling you through God's Emissaries, calling you through the true spiritual teachers that live in the world today, calling you through the great traditions despite the aggregate of their errors and misconceptions.

God has given you Knowledge to guide you, to protect you and to lead you to your greater accomplishments in the world. In this way, God does not have to be something other than God. And you have to live with the reality that there is a greater truth within you—a deeper conscience, a fundamental ethical foundation that cannot be deceived, cannot be corrupted and cannot be used for selfish purposes.

For Knowledge is not a resource of your intellect. Ultimately, your intellect is a resource for Knowledge. But to see this, you would have to shift your sense of identity to a far more permanent and deeper part of your existence to see that your intellect is a magnificent tool of communication. It is there to serve the Spirit, not to imprison the Spirit.

But this revolution within yourself that returns you to your Source and to your true nature is something that most people have not undergone, even amongst those who claim to be religious and religious leaders. They are far too reliant upon their beliefs and their ideas, which does not mean they have traveled far at all on the greater spiritual journey that each person must take.

There is a difference between a scribe and one who is filled with the Spirit of God. Do not judge others in this regard. Everyone is struggling with this to some degree at various different levels of their own self-discovery. Many people have not even begun. Some are struggling at the outset. Others are struggling and trying to find their way as they proceed up this great mountain.

Intellectual brilliance is not the power of Knowledge. Enchanting and fascinating your listeners with eloquence, or a deep study of history, does not represent the greater power of Knowledge within you. Knowledge can speak through a cultivated mind. It can speak through an expanded intellect. And it will do these things according to what is appropriate for your life. But do not confuse the two, as so many people do.

Your soul is lost, but your soul cannot be completely lost because it is tethered to God through Knowledge, through that part of you that never left God. Knowledge, which travels with you every moment, is with you every day in every situation, counseling you and guiding you.

But you cannot feel its counsel or follow its guidance because you are so lost and captivated by the world and by your own internal fantasies and fears, your own internal conflicts, your unforgiveness, your grievances, your attitudes and your fixed beliefs. It is like you are set in a stockade in the center of town, your arms and your head locked in the stockade, and you cannot get out and be in the town because you are stuck there. That is your crown of thorns. That is your imprisonment.

The world celebrates brilliant intellects and artistic talent. It celebrates individual achievement. But it knows not of the power and the presence of Knowledge. It will honor its saints, but only when they are dead and gone, and are no longer a social, political or religious problem.

But people are still able to inspire others because Knowledge is moving through them to a certain extent. Knowledge is everywhere. The demonstrations through selfless giving, the demonstrations through encouragement and inspiration, the demonstrations through countless forms of contribution to the well-being of individuals and to the well-being of nations of people and the whole world are countless and manifest.

You live in a world that is demonstrating Knowledge all the time, and you live in a world that is demonstrating the denial of Knowledge all the time. Where will you place your emphasis then?

That which denies Knowledge is, in essence, evil because it denies the Grace and the Power of God. God will not punish you for these things, but this will deny you the Grace and the Power of God and all of the resolution, comfort and security this will restore to you over time.

The return to God is not simply a decision that you make one day. It is a fundamental change of heart that has to be expressed and demonstrated in many situations, leading to many thresholds of decision. And that is why the progress here is step by step. It is incremental.

God will not let you be close to God because God wants you to be here. The Angels will not let you be close to them because if you become close to them, you will not want to be in this world with all of its difficulties, its fragmented relationships, its problematic human relationships. God wants to turn your eyes to the world, but with the power and the presence of Knowledge to guide you.

Here the Separation, step by step, bit by bit, is reduced. Its power begins to fade. Its influence begins to diminish and is replaced by a greater power that is intrinsic to you and to all people who are here.

A genuine act of kindness can be recognized anywhere, by any culture. You do not have to translate the language. You do not have to understand the culture in all of its dimensions. You do not have to be academic about this. It is simply an act that has universal recognition.

The world is governed by fear—the fear of loss, the fear of losing what one has, the fear of death, the fear of repudiation, the fear of rejection, the fear of expulsion and denial. This is a power that exists in a state of Separation. It is something that is unknown in your Ancient Home.

You cannot return to God at the end of this life because you are not ready. You have not built your capacity for relationship sufficiently. You have not extended your experience of your soul to include others sufficiently yet.

So even if you become a very wise and advanced person in the world, you are given a greater task. Perhaps you will be amongst those who serve those who remain behind. Perhaps you will be sent elsewhere in the universe to serve according to your own lineage and long history. If you achieve any degree of success in terms of the reclamation of Knowledge in your life, God is not going to waste that because your gift grows through contribution. The power of Knowledge grows through contribution. It is not a question of escaping corporeal life. It is a question of service at many, many levels, extending far beyond what your mind can even conceive of at this moment.

What is Hell but having to come back here and do it all over again, or having to go somewhere else which is an even more difficult place to be? To think that you go to Heaven or Hell on the Judgment Day at the end of this life—that is a religion for little children who know nothing of Creation and the Plan of God. Your successes will not be wasted, but will be amplified and expanded in service to the separated that constitute the reality of life in the physical universe.

So you see here, your soul, as it grows, does not diminish. It expands. No longer a single point of light, it now becomes a cluster of lights. It retains some of its uniqueness, but its reality and identity are based upon the strength of its core relationships. Since God is your ultimate relationship, you prepare for God by developing relationships that are genuine and authentic and which serve a greater purpose in your temporary life in the world.

In this regard, Hell is always temporary. The Will of God is to reclaim all of that small part of Creation that has broken away and has lost itself in other realities.

The tragedy is in time. In time, you are suffering. In time, you are losing opportunities. In time, you are failing your mission in being in the world. In time, you are producing more suffering for others and more suffering for yourself as a result—compounding your problem, deepening your dilemma, further darkening your mind.

There are certainly worse Hells than this. Humanity is remarkable in the degree of suffering it can generate for itself, both individually and collectively. God will reclaim you in the end, but the end can be a long time from now, and you are suffering in time. You are languishing in time.

Your soul cannot reunite without the reclamation of Knowledge. That part of you which is wise must guide that part of you which is foolish. That part of you that has not become separate from God must guide that part of you that still thinks it is in Separation from God.

In this way, God does not have to exert special effort for your salvation because the process is already underway. God does not have to be your therapist, your counselor or your personal attendant, nor even the Angelic Presence. People think the Angelic Presence is again like their bed maiden, their personal attendants. This, of course, is ridiculous.

The Unseen Ones, the Angelic Presence that might counsel you on occasion, have thousands of individuals they have to look after. They are not going to dally around with you and your foolishness. But they will respond to those moments when your mind stirs and greater possibilities emerge for you.

Your soul then becomes greater, more expansive and more inclusive of others as you advance and as you make progress in your spiritual development. You no longer live just for yourself. You live also for others and for their well-being. Perhaps your sense of others includes just your family, but it can include other people. It can include larger panoramas of relationship, dealing with neighborhoods and communities. There are even certain individuals who look at humanity as their fundamental relationship. But this is a very advanced state and is only meant for certain people whose contribution has to function within a very large arena.

Your greater purpose in the world is not your invention, and you cannot come to it on your own terms. It must be revealed to you, and you must be willing for this revelation to take place and to have the patience and the humility to be able to receive this progressively, for you cannot face it all at once.

Here you realize that your mind is not your greater reality though you have allowed it to dominate you and control you, and you have identified with it inappropriately. It is still part of your existence in the world. It still distinguishes you in many ways. It is still the avenue for your innate talents to express themselves in relationship to others. But you are listening for a greater power now.

This power comes from both within and from beyond. Messages can be sent into your mind through the Angelic Presence, but what is most important is that Knowledge within you confirms these things.

Knowledge is really the focal point. It is not even God. You cannot focus on God. You can focus on your ideas about God or your belief about God, but what is this?

You experience God through a deeper connection within yourself, a deeper connection with others and a deeper connection with Unseen Forces in the universe that are really guiding the currents of your life.

Your mind is like the ocean at the surface—turbulent and unpredictable, pointless, whipped by the winds of the world, one day calm, one day turbulent. You look at the surface and you cannot make any sense out of it. It has no certain direction except when you see that it is governed by tides, which are governed by celestial forces beyond the range of your personal experience. But even beyond this, the ocean itself has deeper currents that move the waters of the world all over the planet, governed by greater forces than the winds of the world.

You see, your mind is whipped by the winds of the world. You are happy. You are sad. You are turbulent. You are inconsistent. You suffer over meaningless things. You pursue meaningless things. You are in conflict with yourself and other people. You do not know what you are doing or what you want—profoundly confused, profoundly conflicted. It is a mess. Do you think God is going to work this out for you?

God just pulls you away from it. And along the way, you clean up the mess. You bridge the gap of unforgiveness with yourself and others. You make amends. You alter your course. You change your behavior. You alter your ideas. You even change your whole notion of yourself.

If people are not willing to do this, then nothing happens. They can be priests. They can be governors. They can be presidents. They can be kings. They can proclaim anything, but they are no more than what they have created within themselves. Without Knowledge, this is nothing—a racket, an empty gesture, someone crying in the wind, forgotten, insignificant.

But your life is significant. You have not been forgotten, and God has spoken again to reveal the true nature of the soul and its redemption. This is at the heart of all the world's religions, but what is at the heart can be concealed by what is in the mind.

Many people need this clarification, within their faith traditions and those who have no faith tradition. For humanity is facing the great change that is coming to the world—great difficulties and great challenges. These things can call out of you your true gifts and your deeper nature if you know how to respond to them. But to respond, you must recognize them and prepare for them. And for this you will need the assistance of the Creator, for humanity is unaware and unprepared.

When you leave this world, your soul will be different from what you think it is now. When you advance, and your mind expands, and the soul expands to become a cluster of lights instead of a singular light, the definition and the experience of the soul will be very different.

Let this be your understanding.

CHAPTER 7

WHAT CREATES EVIL?

As revealed to
Marshall Vian Summers
on January 17, 2008
in Boulder, Colorado

One must come to realize in being in the world that there are destructive forces within the world. If one is really honest and self-observant, one will realize that there are even destructive forces within oneself. Certainly, within the world around you, these destructive forces become evident and have been a part of human experience throughout its entire history.

If you are observant of your own thoughts and inclinations, it will be apparent to you that there are destructive forces within you. You see this in your desire for revenge. You see this in your desire to conquer or overwhelm others. You see this in your desires, however secret they might be, to remove or eliminate other people. You see this in your dreams.

You see this even in your desire to change the world. For how can you change the world without removing those or eliminating those or silencing those who would oppose you? This is a fundamental problem of being within a physical reality, of living within a body and competing for resources with others who are in the physical reality and who are living in bodies.

The great Separation that has set in motion the existence and expansion of the universe was not created out of an evil intention.

It was not a mistake. It was not born of evil. But within this compromised existence, evil becomes inevitable.

It is not a force that is generated by one mythological individual— someone fell from grace and became the source and the center of evil. This is certainly not the case when you think of yourself living within a Greater Community of intelligent life in the universe, where there are countless races, so unlike you, living within very different environments, representing all stages of psychological, mental and technological evolution. Clearly, it is not one individual who is the source of everyone's problems. Rather, it is the result of living within a compromised, separated existence.

Therefore, you cannot blame the existence of evil on any individual. It is the product of living within your current condition, which does not represent your existence in your Ancient Home, the existence from which you have come and to which you will return.

You have come from a reality where you are known and there are no questions into a reality where you are not known and where there are only questions, and very few real answers. You have come from a place of total security and inclusion to a place without security and that demonstrates Separation everywhere. You have come from a place where you were at peace now to a place where you must survive and compete, where you must navigate uncertain conditions and ever-changing circumstances. It is entirely different being in the physical reality, being in a body.

The Angelic Host that represents the Creator of all life serve as intermediaries between your Ancient Home and your current reality—living within the physical existence, living in the body and having to deal with this kind of reality, which is so very different from where you have come from.

Here God seems to be mysterious. God does not seem to be present. God is nowhere to be found. You are living an existence where God does not seem to exist even at all, unless one has great faith. How very different this is from where you have come from and that Home to which you will return.

And coming [from] within this environment, your ideas of God are so limited. People think that God is like them—very powerful, of course, very wise, of course, but judgmental and vengeful and angry and frustrated, just like they are. They have created God in their own image.

Therefore, any appreciation of God is only an approximation. There is no absolute truth about God born out of your current existence because your current existence is not absolute. It is a relative reality, relative in that it is moving and changing and that it has a beginning and an end. Yet where you have come from is not changing. It does not have a beginning and an end. It is not in flux. It is not uncertain. It is not unpredictable.

Therefore, it is important to consider here that the existence of evil is the result of living within this condition. It is inevitable. If you take away a being's sense of inclusion and their security and you throw them into an environment where they must now survive and compete, where they must destroy other organisms in order to survive, where they must constantly deal with uncertainty and the risk of destruction and where deprivation is ever present and always a continuous threat, how can you expect them to function in a state of absolute wisdom and compassion, without fear or anxiety attending them at every turn?

God does not expect this. God does not expect one to be perfect within these circumstances, for no one will be perfect, and God does not expect what cannot be. You might expect this of yourself and other people, but that is because you do not understand the reality into which you have entered and for which you have chosen to come.

Therefore, God does not punish evil because evil is inevitable. It is like punishing a child for being childish. It is like punishing a fool for being foolish. There is no punishment of evil. Evil only perpetuates one's misery and makes the possibility of redemption delayed and more remote.

People have trouble accepting this, of course, because they want God to take revenge for them. Unable or unwilling to exact the punishment they think must be rendered themselves, now they want God to do it for them. This again is the result of creating God in one's own image, a God like them, just more powerful, that is all.

Hell is an invention that people have created to punish those whom they hate and cannot stand. But you are already living in a kind of Hell, you see, the Hell of Separation. To commit yourself more deeply to this condition represents a further descent into Hell. To isolate yourself further, governed now only by your fearful imagination and your condemnation of yourself, others and the world, plunges you further into a condition that is by its nature fundamentally difficult.

So evil is all around you. It is a force. It takes the form of forces in the mental environment, forces of persuasion, forces you cannot see, but that you can feel, which affect your thinking, your emotions and your behavior.

You see, that is why individuals, groups and entire nations can commit themselves to actions that are fundamentally destructive and counter-productive. A whole nation can commit itself to invading and destroying another nation for its wealth and its resources under pretenses of national security or self-preservation. Or it [war] can be waged under the banner of religion, thinking that the other nation is impious or evil, that they are pagans, the unredeemed. But this is all just an excuse for expressing the power and the force of evil. And though it might be led by a few determined individuals, everyone else will be swept along.

How can this be? How can such a force have such influence? It is power, you see, in the mental environment.

In order to survive in this world, you need assistance and support, and to gain that assistance and support, you will make many compromises—in your relationships with others, in your marriages, all around you in all your relationships, in your relationship with the nation in which you live. You want its assistance, protection and approval, so you will go along with it, even if it is doing something that is heinous and clearly a violation of what you most truly value.

This is the power of evil functioning in the mental environment, expressing itself within a social context. It can be disguised as duty to one's nation or one's family that can lead you to do things that are clearly in violation of what Knowledge within you would indicate— the deeper intelligence that the Creator of all life has placed within you. A violation of Knowledge, a violation of God, a violation of what you know to be right—you will violate these to gain the assistance, protection and approval that you think are necessary for your survival. This is a real predicament. It is again a predicament of living within this separated existence.

The world is a beautiful place. It is marvelous. It is Creation happening every moment. It is change happening every moment. If you can stand apart from this and experience it—without fearing for your own survival, without being afraid of what you might lose or have to give up—it can actually be a marvelous experience. But do not confuse it with your Ancient Home from which you have come and to which you will return. There is no comparison.

Therefore, you must accept the world as it is. You cannot make it like your Ancient Home. Even God cannot make it like your Ancient Home, for God made it to be something different.

God is not the author of evil, but God has created an environment where evil, at least among intelligent races who are aware of their own mortality, will be likely and inevitable. But God has given an antidote to evil, a powerful antidote it is, placed within you in the power and the presence of Knowledge, a deeper mind within you. Not the mind that you think with. Not the mind that judges and speculates, compares and condemns, but a deeper mind—a mind like the Mind of God; a mind that does not think like your personal mind thinks; a mind that sees, waits, knows and acts with power and commitment.

This is the antidote, you see. It is the antidote to evil within yourself, and the persuasions of evil within yourself and all around you, which are so prevalent and powerful in the world. It is ultimately an antidote to evil throughout the universe. But it must become strong within individuals.

The power of Knowledge within you is incorruptible. It is not persuaded or affected by the seductions and inducements within the human world and even within the Greater Community, where the expression of evil and conflict has been in existence for so very long.

You, on your own, cannot combat evil. If you tried to combat it, it would seduce you. You will become more like it. It will turn you from being a peaceful advocate into being a warrior yourself. You will find yourself taking up arms against others whom you consider to be governed by evil.

You will become like them because evil loves the attention. It thrives off of human engagement. It is empowered by those who follow it and by those who are opposed to it. For without human allegiance and human attention, evil has nowhere to attach itself. Those who are committed to it need allegiance and need engagement from others.

There are very few people in the world who are really evil, who have committed themselves to this force, this power. But their influence on society at large is tremendous. Their destructive impact is tremendous. The effects of their actions upon others, given their numbers, are tremendous. The force of their persuasions to engage nations in war with other nations is very powerful, you see.

You as an individual cannot combat this without risking falling under its persuasions and its inducements. To try to do this is to commit yourself to being in opposition to others. It places you and pits you against others fundamentally, even from the outset. Now you must fight others to do and to create what you think is right.

While it is fine to oppose others for a good cause, in this circumstance, it changes your intentions. It changes your motivations because you are governed by fear—the fear of failure, the fear of not achieving what you want to achieve, the fear of thinking that if you are not successful, the opposing forces will be supreme. Fear gives rise to anger. Anger gives rise to hatred. Hatred gives rise to violence. And violence gives rise to further violence.

This is a trap, you see. It is a fundamental conundrum. It takes good people and places them in opposition to one another, alters their true intentions to establish peace and cooperation and manifests entirely different results.

There is a greater Wisdom living within you that is not affected by forces of dissonance within the world, by the persuasions of others or by the inducements of culture or even religion. It is free. It is pure. It is clear. It is answerable only to God because it is an extension of God.

No matter how far you go in trying to establish your isolation, in trying to be successful in Separation and in trying to make Separation work, you are still connected to God through Knowledge, this deeper mind within you. You cannot escape from it. You cannot divorce yourself from it. You can deny it. You can cover its light with many covers and live in darkness, but you cannot eliminate it. It represents your purpose for being in the world, your connection to God and your redemption.

The question is: How long will it take for you to come to desire it and to realize that without it, you cannot be successful, you cannot fulfill yourself, and you cannot make a real contribution to the world, which is your real intention for being here? Without it, you cannot fulfill the need of your soul. Without it, you cannot have peace and integrity within yourself. Without it, you cannot have a successful relationship with yourself, or with other people or even with the whole world.

You may still believe in the power of the military, the power of weapons, the power of force, the power of government, the power of personal persuasion, the power of personal dominance, the power of wealth, the power of beauty or the power of cleverness and charm, but only Knowledge within you has the real power to reunite, to reconnect, to bless and to inspire.

The world has established its own gods, its own definitions, its own expressions of power and dominance, persuasion and conquest and so forth. But Knowledge within you and within others is not fooled by this.

You cannot make Knowledge give you what you want, for it is more powerful than you are, than your personal mind—a mind full of desire and conflict, fear and apprehension, a mind that is identified with everything that is uncertain, a mind that is subject to the power of evil, a mind that is easily influenced and has been influenced.

But deeper within you is Knowledge. You have what is unchanged, you see. It is coming back to what is unchanged within you that is your redemption, that is your power, that begins to free you from the grip of addiciton and the grip of persuasion.

You can pretend to be anyone you want to try to be. You can give yourself any name. You can establish yourself in any role. You can play the role of the good person or the bad person. But within you, there is Knowledge, waiting to be discovered.

CHAPTER 8

THE REDEMPTION

As revealed to
Marshall Vian Summers
on July 8, 2013
in Boulder, Colorado

Only God knows the way to God. Only God knows what redemption means, what it will require and how it must be achieved. People, of course, have very fixed notions upon this based upon the earlier Revelations that have been so altered by man over time. But this cannot be fully comprehended by anyone on Earth, for it is far too complex. It deals with realities of which you are unaware. It deals with the reality of Creation, of which you are unaware. It deals with your origin and your destiny, of which you are unaware. It deals with those who sent you into the world and who will receive you when you leave, of which you are unaware.

It is not possible for humanity to fully comprehend this, or any race in the universe for that matter, for they are all living in Separation. But certain things can be clarified and the pathway can be made evident, where it has been glossed over or confused in the past.

That is what We shall give today. It is not a complete understanding, for you cannot have that. Your mind is not big enough, your worldly mind, that is. Yet the deeper Knowledge that God has put within you can resonate with this naturally, without effort, for it is still part of Creation even if you are wandering in the physical universe.

What is redemption? Redemption means, in the context of your life, returning to your natural Self, returning to your deeper awareness, returning to your connection with God and what God has sent you into the world to do. It is to re-establish fundamentally your connection with the deeper Knowledge that God has placed within you—to guide you and to protect you and to lead you to a greater life, a greater life which you have not yet discovered.

When you think about this, you will realize how absolutely essential it is to your happiness, to your fulfillment and to the meaning and quality of your life and everything you do here. For without a greater destiny and a purpose in the world, you are adrift. Like a speck on the ocean, you are adrift. Even if you have wealth and splendor and seem to be marginally in control of your life, you are still adrift internally. You are a stranger to yourself. You do not know where you have come from or where you are going. You do not know what you are really here to do, despite all of your goals and plans.

It is really a terrible situation if you look at it honestly and objectively. Because people do not look at this honestly and objectively, they are constantly running away from themselves—staying busy, preoccupied, distracted, chasing dreams, chasing romance, chasing wealth, and if they have any wealth at all, an endless shopping spree in life, filling their life with ever more things to encumber them and to bog them down.

We are speaking of something that is essential to every person, regardless of their religion, regardless of their social status, regardless of their nation or culture, regardless of their history, even regardless of how they might view themselves. The elemental truth of your existence is the same.

Living in Separation, you think that everyone has a unique path. Everyone is unique. They even have a unique relationship with God. But, of course, nobody really knows what this means. Though it might be comforting in the moment, though it might drive off insecurity and give you a sense of control, it is inherently false and illusory.

We are speaking of that which is central to your life and to everything you do—to the meaning of your relationships and whether they are authentic and purposeful or not, to the meaning of your mind as a vehicle of communication in the world and to the meaning of your body as a vehicle of communication in the world.

In fact, when you come into the proximity of Knowledge and the power of redemption that lives within you, everything has a new meaning. Everything begins to make sense. The confusion you have lived with, the confusion which you even defend through your ideas and beliefs, begins slowly to be dispelled, like a fog burning off the landscape, revealing everything that was concealed before.

Only God knows the way, and God has put the power of Knowledge within you. In fact, this power of Knowledge has been with you since the beginning, for it represents the part of you that has never left God, that is still connected to Creation. It is the only part of you that is fearless. It is the only part of you that cannot be corrupted or seduced. It is the only part of you that is truly trustworthy in this regard.

That which is weak within you, which is your personal mind and all of the compromises you have made—your fear, your condemnation of others, your anger, your resentment, your unforgiveness—all of this represents but the surface of your mind, polluted from being in the world and from your own errant decisions and the persuasions of others.

God has put a power within you that is beyond all this, which is meant to guide you in all things, to lead you forward when that is needed, and to hold you back when that is necessary. How clear this is, how simple it is, and yet to your intellect, it is confusing because your intellect only understands reality in terms of Separation. It cannot conceive of your Heavenly Home. It cannot conceive of Creation, where the one are many and the many are one. It cannot conceive of anything beyond what the senses have reported in this world. So it is incapable of understanding Knowledge.

But that is not necessary. In fact, it is impossible. God will redeem you as you learn to discover the power and presence that lives within you and begin to follow it and to allow it to reshape your life according to your true purpose and your deeper nature. In this, you begin to feel you have a true design for being in the world. And with the discovery of your design, you begin to recall the reality of your Designer.

If you can accept that your life exists beyond the realm of your intellect—your ideas, your beliefs, your plans, your goals and all the superficial aspects of your personality—then you begin to find a greater strength, a greater permanence and with it increasing freedom from fear and anxiety. For you become anchored in a deeper part of yourself that is not afraid and knows what must be done.

This does not happen all at once. You take the Steps to Knowledge. You learn to readjust your ideas. You learn to temper your passions. You learn to see things with clear eyes, to open your ears so you can listen inside, to clear your vision so you can see others without judgment, condemnation and comparison. Your mind becomes refreshed. Your mind becomes renewed. And the darkness of your past and all of the shadows that follow you and have followed you begin to dissipate as you take these Steps to Knowledge.

God is very intelligent. God does not have to figure out your dilemma. God just calls you, and your dilemma falls apart. God does not have to figure out all of your intricate problems and the complexity of your ideas, for God calls you, and something greater within you responds.

But to follow this response, you must have an adequate degree of self-trust and self-appreciation, qualities that unfortunately many people seem to lack. They have been so degraded living in Separation. Degraded by their compromises, by their indulgences and by the persuasions of others, they have no real regard for themselves, even to the point of being disgusted with themselves.

So here it is more difficult, for you must give yourself the credit that you require to even begin. For you must now trust something within that is not based on your ideas or your past experiences, something intrinsic to you, something that God has put there like a beacon—calling you, calling you, holding you back, keeping you from destroying your life or going so far off course that within this life nothing can bring you back.

You may be a speck on the ocean, but God knows your heart and your mind and speaks to you from within you at a level that you have rarely ever experienced. This is redemption at work, step by step, increment by increment, day by day. Emotionally, you go up and down, going from joy to fear to anxiety to self-doubt to exhaustion. But like the clouds obscuring the heavens above, there is a greater Presence there that is always with you. It is your connection to God.

God is much greater than this, of course. You can never call yourself God, but you are connected to God at this level only. Here the intellect can only follow and serve, to be a servant of a greater master, for Knowledge is the master. In this regard, there are no masters living in the world. Liberate yourself from such notions. You cannot attain mastery. You can become skillful, but the master is greater than your mind, always. The master is the part of you that is connected to God.

Here war and violence cease to be an emphasis for you. Here forgiveness and reconciliation take the place of hatred and vengeance. For Knowledge within you is in harmony with Knowledge within others, even within your enemies, even within those who have hurt you or have committed crimes against your people or nation.

There is no enmity in Knowledge. The things that are grievous within you and all around you are the product of living in Separation. God knew these things would arise. God knew that living in Separation, evil would have a force and a power in your life and would exist in the world, for it is the result of living in Separation—a Separation that you and countless others chose long before this life and existence.

God is not going to punish you for this because you had the freedom to live in Separation, and you exercised that. Now with this freedom, you must find the return. For life here without Knowledge, purpose, meaning and true relationship is miserable, confused and hopeless. If you have the self-honesty to recognize this, then you will begin to see and to recognize the great gift that the Lord of the universe is providing to you now through a New Revelation for humanity. The gift of Knowledge was part of all the previous Revelations, but has been lost and obscured through human adoption and misuse.

You may pray to God. You may believe in God. You may bow down to God. You may think that God is guiding every little thing in your life. But God has set in motion the forces of the world at the beginning of time. God has put Knowledge within you now to guide you. If you do not honor this, then your prayers and your bowing down to God will have no meaning, for you will not be following what God has given you to follow, which is mysterious and must be discovered through self-honesty and a deeper reckoning within yourself.

This will all take time, of course, but to God time is nothing. But to you, time is everything—your time, this time, the time you have left on Earth, the time you have wasted and lost, the time you have in this moment, the time before you now. What will you do with this? Live in the memories of the past? Continue to chase illusions? Try to make something of your life for the approval of others or to satisfy and try to alleviate yourself from the suffering that exists within you, the suffering of Separation?

You may think you are happy. You may think your life is okay. But if you sit quietly, if you can sit quietly and be present to yourself, you will see that this is only an excuse, something you tell yourself. There are happy moments. There are pleasurable encounters. There are beautiful places and things to enjoy. But we are speaking of something much deeper, much more pervasive. It is the foundation upon which you stand.

God knows your only foundation in this world, in this life, in the physical universe itself, is the foundation of Knowledge. Everything else is weak and subject to change and destruction, and that is why you live in constant fear and apprehension. If you are not deluding yourself, you will see that this is the case and will seek to find relief from it.

God knows that not everyone can follow the same religion. God knows that not everyone can follow the same great Teacher or Messenger. God knows that not everyone is going to agree about the principles of religion, or even the ideas and beliefs about God. So that is hopeless. The world can never become united, whole and complete at that level. It must happen at a deeper, more profound aspect of yourself.

People pray to God for many things. They want relief from their difficulties. They want success for themselves or those they care about. They might even pray for the well-being of others that they do not know, or for peace on Earth. This can be very authentic and can represent a true response. But you still must find that within you that holds redemption for you.

You cannot find it through the scriptures. You cannot find it through the great texts or the sacred places. For all these can do is bring you back to that essential aspect that lives within you, that is still connected to God, that holds the power of redemption and the journey that you must take towards redemption in your life, wherever you are in life. Even if you are at the beginning of life or the middle or towards the end, it is the same.

Heaven only knows what Heaven has created in you. What you have made of yourself is something else. But what Heaven has created in you is the essential part of you. It is who you were before you came into the world. It will be who you are when you leave this world and return to those who watch over you. Here your beliefs are not important. They are only valued in terms of whether they brought you to Knowledge or not.

In a universe of a billion, billion, billion races and more, God has set the power of redemption. It was begun at the beginning of time, the beginning of the Separation, for you can never leave Creation completely. You can never leave God completely. You can never leave your Source completely. Even if you have led a degraded and pathetic life—even a violent life—you still cannot leave that which is your center and your Source. So it is all a matter of time when you will return to that which calls to you, which is waiting for you, even at this moment.

But religion has confused this terribly—religious belief and understanding; and human conjecture, human adoption and human corruption. So now the stream is very muddy and very unclear, and the waters are not pure. So God has brought the pure waters of Revelation again into the world, after such a very long time, at a time when humanity is standing at the precipice of a radically changing and degrading world, at a time when humanity is standing at the threshold of engaging with life in the universe within a Greater Community of life, of which you know nothing at all.

It is this great time of Revelation where the reality of redemption must be clarified and purified, where the Revelation itself must be given in a pure form during the life of the Messenger, who has been assigned from the Angelic Assembly to bring it here. It is at this time that these things must become clear.

For religion now has collapsed into contention and conflict, internally and between its great traditions. Humanity is entering a world of diminishing resources and growing population. How will you find reconciliation and cooperation in such a world? Only God knows the moment that Revelation must be given and what it must be saying and what it must give and what it must correct.

This is before you now—the greatest Revelation ever given to this world, given to a world now of global commerce and communication and growing global awareness. You are no longer isolated, primitive tribes of people. You now must take responsibility for the welfare of the world and for the welfare of human civilization.

What will give you the strength, clarity and wisdom to do this? Despite all of the issues and contentions and disagreements that exist everywhere, what will give you the power to do this? Only God knows. Only God can give the answer. And God has given the answer. You carry it within you like a flame, beyond the realm of your intellect, beyond the realm of your ideas and preoccupations. You are like a deep ocean, but you only live at the surface, unaware of what exists down below.

The power of Knowledge works within each person, within their circumstances, giving them the strength to make the clear decisions that must be made to bring their life in order, to return to the integrity and the strength that abide within them, to pull away from unhealthy influences and relationships and to regain their strength, regardless of their circumstances.

Knowledge works within each person in different ways, but all for the same purpose and goal, you see. That is why there is no conflict between Knowledge in one and Knowledge in another. Thus, it is the great peacemaker. It is the power that will give humanity the strength to restore the world and to establish a future unlike the past. It is the most powerful force in the universe—more powerful than great technological societies, which are so tragic in the repression of their peoples and populations.

God's New Revelation gives you the chance to see the universe, to see your world and to see yourself with such clarity. But it will be a different experience. It may stand in great contrast to your beliefs and ideas and the beliefs and ideas of your culture, your society, your family and so forth. For God's Redemption is not what people think it is because people really do not know.

God has given you the pathway, the Steps to Knowledge. God has given you the strength and the return to your strength. God has given you a world to serve, which will take you out of your personal misery and confusion and set you on a path of restoration, integrity and service. For this is why you have come, you see—not to languish in a declining world, but to provide a unique service to the people of this world. Only Knowledge really knows what this is. It is not what you think.

We are giving you the greatest secret in the universe—the key. But you must practice to comprehend. You must take the journey to understand what it really means. You cannot sit on the sidelines and try to figure this out. That is hopeless and foolish. If you dismiss this, then you are merely demonstrating your ignorance and foolishness.

You must come to the Revelation to see it. You must follow it to understand it. You must experience Knowledge to know that it is real within you and is not a product of your imagination, something you have constructed for yourself.

The blessing is upon the world, for the Messenger is here. The Revelation has come into the world. It brings with it power, integrity and the spirit of service and contribution. It is unlike anything that God has presented before, for God must speak to the whole world now, and time is of the essence because humanity is degrading the world so severely that it will determine the fate of human civilization. Humanity is facing Intervention from the universe and is unprepared. These are the greatest events in human history, but people are unaware. They are living in a dream.

It is a time of the greatest importance. It is the time you have chosen to be here. It is the time when your contribution must be discovered, honestly. It is the time of Revelation.

Your redemption is fulfilled through your contribution to the world and through your alignment with Knowledge because the closer you become to Knowledge and the closer that you follow Knowledge, the more your engagement with the Source of your life and with all of Creation is strengthened in your experience. Though you will continue to have moments of great doubt and uncertainty, great fear and apprehension, the strength of your connection will be growing as you take each step towards Knowledge.

This is how you are redeemed—by reclaiming and regaining your relationship with your Source, not through belief or ideology, but by adhering to the power that God has put within you to follow. You regain your strength and you overcome your weakness by following this, by holding yourself back when that is necessary and by sending yourself forth where it is necessary.

It is a perfect Plan, beyond human comprehension. It is a Plan that is set in motion for all the races in the universe. How can anyone understand a Plan of this magnitude and this degree of inclusion? What could serve races of beings from such different worlds, different cultures, different religions who appear so different from one another and yet be a Plan so perfect that it works in all situations?

It is as if your personality and body were like costumes that you put on and you become so identified with them. But when you take them off, you are still all the same, you see. Back in the dressing room beyond this world, well, there you are.

But what happens after life is not important now. God will not send you to Hell. What is important now is what you serve, what you follow and what directs your life, now and tomorrow and the days to come. That is what is important. That is what will fulfill you if you can follow it, or that which will leave you in confusion and shadow if you cannot.

God will not punish you, but you can still live in misery, as you have done so before. God is giving you a way out of misery—not a way out of the world, but a way out of misery—by giving you the pathway to re-engage with the Source of your life and to bring your soul back to union with the deeper part of you that has never left God. This is the redemption.

CHAPTER 9

GOD, KNOWLEDGE AND THE ANGELIC PRESENCE

As revealed to
Marshall Vian Summers
on September 17, 2008
in Boulder, Colorado

The universe is immense, so immense that it is incomprehensible. No one has been able to travel its lengths. No one has been able to encompass its vastness and complexity. It is beyond the intellectual grasp of any race in the universe. Yet the entire Creation has one Source and one Author.

When you begin to think of God within this larger context, God becomes so vast and immense as to be incomprehensible. And certainly you must relinquish the idea that God is preoccupied with any one world, with any one race of beings.

Throughout human history, man's relationship to God has been the center point of religious studies and focus. But here, for the most part, God is conceived of as a very local entity—a being with human values, a being who is imbued with the psychology and the emotions of a human being. Even if God is considered to be incomprehensible, God is still imbued with human values, human emotions and human psychology.

To think of God beyond this limited definition, one would have to reconsider one's own nature, one's own future, one's own destiny and one's entire reality. It [God] could not be bound to this Earth alone. If you are God's Creation, part of God's Creation, then you are connected to all of Creation, not to this one little world, which is like a grain of sand in a beach that stretches as far as the eye can see.

Whenever history or legend speaks of God speaking to the people, or God being angry with human behavior, or disappointed with humanity's existence, one is imbuing God with human attributes and considering God only within the context of this one world.

But the Creator of all life is the Creator of all life—life that is so very different from the human form and from human consciousness. Intelligent life has evolved throughout the universe, in countless forms, with very different expressions. Yet they are all subject to the forces of nature in this physical reality. They all require resources and a supportive environment. They all must struggle with provisioning themselves and their worlds. And they all face demise because they are living a temporary life in a physical reality.

To even begin to consider God within this vast arena of intelligent life, one must reconsider one's whole idea of God and see that God really extends far beyond human estimation and that the stories about God, the legends about God and the history of human thought about God must necessarily be very, very limited—limited to your experience and awareness and to the limits of your immediate environment.

God of a Greater Community of life is very different. God is not preoccupied with human affairs.

Over the course of time, God has sent Messengers into the world, Messengers who have been sent here by the Angelic Presence that oversees this world's evolution and well-being.

God is too big to be concerned with this one world. God is not a human being. God is not limited by human understanding, human psychology or human emotions.

The Plan of redemption for all separated beings living in the physical reality extends to all dimensions, and this Plan encompasses a vast network of support for those still living in form—living in a physical reality, caught in identity in a separate reality.

To understand God's Work in the world, you must understand God's Work in the entire universe. Many people think that the universe is just a big empty place. But it is full of life, and the dimensions and the expanse of this life are unimaginable.

Yet God is everywhere, redeeming the separated through Knowledge through a deeper intelligence that God has placed within all sentient beings. Instead of God watching over your life, or sending you messages, or being displeased with your apparent lack of progress, God has just put Knowledge within you to guide you, to lead you and to restrain you.

People are living at the surface of their mind—in their intellect, in the part of the mind that is a product of social conditioning. They do not feel the power and the presence of Knowledge. Perhaps they have an intuition once in a while, deeper feelings that they cannot account for, strange premonitions or a sense of foreboding and restraint.

Everyone has had this experience to some degree, and this is the evidence of a deeper current of your life, a deeper mind beneath the surface mind where you live. Beyond your identity of yourself as an individual; beyond your social, political and religious conditioning, there is this deeper mind.

God has given you this mind. In fact, this mind is who you really are. It is not limited by the conditions of this world, by the errors of human behavior or by the powers of persuasion that exist here and anywhere in the universe. It is the most important part of you. Yet it is the part of you that is least explored, least experienced and least understood.

God has assigned to each world where sentient beings live, or have colonized, a force of redemption for these nations and groups of individuals. In worlds such as yours, which are largely inhabited, where there is a great diversity and complexity of life, this Angelic Presence has many different levels of expression and different levels of service. Yet its overall purpose is to oversee the progress and the well-being of humanity.

But the Angelic Presence cannot interfere uninvited unless they are requested with great earnestness to be of assistance. Even here there are limitations placed because you have been given a free will living in this separated state—living in form, now unaware of your origin and your destiny, now unaware of the greater Knowledge that lives within you.

You are given free will—the freedom to choose, the freedom to deny, the freedom to deceive yourself and others, the freedom to believe whatever you want, to imagine whatever you want, to think of God and reality in any way you want, or not at all. You have this freedom. Therefore, the Angelic Presence must respect this freedom.

Many people want God to return or come again, to overtake the world, punish the wicked and elevate the righteous. But this is not going to happen. People are expecting the second coming of the emancipator, in whatever form or personage they can imagine, and they think this will lead to a great era of peace and righteousness. But that is not going to happen.

Humanity's success and failure are largely in its hands. But the Angelic Presence is here to encourage and to stimulate those individuals who are open to its Presence, who are willing to follow its recommendations and to live a more ethical and purposeful life based on service to humanity and to this world. All others who seek the Angelic Presence to enrich themselves, to gain advantage over others or to destroy their enemies will find no response and no assistance.

If you want God's help, you must earnestly seek it, and you must not have any other expectations or incentives. God is not in the business of enriching certain people and impoverishing everyone else. The condition of the world is a condition that humanity has created for itself, within the limits and the restraints of the environment of this world.

You have free will, even if you do not feel free, even if you are politically unfree or socially not free. You can still choose what to follow, what to believe in, what to value and what to deny. It is to encourage choosing in the right direction, choosing in the direction of your own redemption and self-realization, that the Angelic Presence is here to encourage you.

Beyond this, they do not interfere, despite all the stories of God intervening on behalf of certain peoples at certain times. This represents a misunderstanding of God's Plan and the purpose and the power of the Angelic Presence here.

Throughout the universe, there are countless Beings in the Angelic Presence who are serving those still living in a separated state to encourage their connection to the deeper Knowledge that God has placed within them, and through this Knowledge, to bring benefit and progress, peace and tolerance into these nations, where in so many cases it has been lost, suppressed or forgotten.

There are very few free nations in the universe because freedom is chaotic and disruptive. It is creative. It knows no bounds. And so for many races, they have chosen to eliminate it or to limit it to a great degree in order to achieve social order and stability, thus limiting themselves, their progress in life and their ability to gain access to Knowledge and all of the powers and skills it will provide, for the individual and for nations as a whole.

For when you cease to be creative, you cease to advance and progress. But many worlds and many nations have chosen this. And humanity is at great risk of choosing this pathway, valuing and worshiping its technology and forgetting where the power of inspiration and creativity really comes from.

The Angelic Presence that is here will respond to the yearning of the heart and the soul. They will respond to what is truly being communicated and expressed through your requests and through your prayers. You may think you want your business to work, or for some outcome to happen for a certain person, but really it is often about something else. For at the basis of your request is the desire to be reconnected to the power and presence of God within yourself, and the Power and Presence of God that exists within this world—in people and beyond people, all the way into the Angelic Presence.

You may ask God for a favor or a miracle, but the deeper request really is to become connected because once you are connected to Knowledge within yourself, then God can speak to you through Knowledge. The Will of God speaks to you. It is not as if God leaves the universe and comes to whisper in your ears. It is the Will and the

Intention of God, directed by the Angelic Presence here on Earth, that communicates to you through Knowledge.

People may be very confused about what Knowledge is because they are thinking of it in terms of psychology or their understanding of religion. But essentially, Knowledge is the deeper mind within you, through which God's Will can communicate to you and guide you.

God has imbued you with a deeper conscience—far deeper and more pervasive this is than your social conscience, which has been established by your family, your society and your religious training, if you have had religious training. There is a deeper sense of what is right and wrong, what is true and untrue, what is just and what is unjust, that goes beyond your social conditioning and the expectations of others.

The fact that very few people have experienced this to any great degree represents the limits of humanity's progress, showing that humanity has not really progressed that far in its overall evolution—in the evolution of its awareness and its greater strength. You may have weapons of mass destruction, you may have invented some unique and clever devices in your technology, but most people still do not have any idea of who they are or where they are going in life. That is all left up to ideology, social convention or pure fantasy.

So overall humanity has not progressed very far. But your progress, individually and as a whole, is very important, and it is this that the Angelic Presence supports. What is this support for? It is primarily for the emergence of Knowledge within the individual, and the strength and power of Knowledge within humanity as a whole.

Humanity's understanding of God's Plan and Presence is really limited. It is very local. It assumes that God is just a big person, with all the feelings and tendencies of a person. God is a big human being—very powerful of course, very wise of course. But most people think of God personally in this way, someone they can relate to who understands their problems and difficulties.

When your history or your legends speak of God communicating to the world, what is really being described here is the Angelic Presence communicating to certain individuals. A sacred book, for example, if it is claimed that it comes from God or is the Word of God, is actually the words of the Angelic Presence. For God does not use words to communicate. With an infinite number of languages in the universe, God does not use your particular language to communicate. That all comes from the Angelic Presence that is assigned to the well-being of your particular world.

The Will of God flows through the Angelic Presence, and all the levels of the Angelic Presence, and flows through Knowledge within the individual and expresses itself there. Just like life force expresses itself in the plants and the animals, with each beat of your heart, and each breath that you take, God's Will permeates everything—finding avenues of expression, translating through levels of relationships.

Here the Angelic Presence serves as an intermediary between the pure experience and reality of God and your individual separated life here in the world. The Angelic Presence translates God's Will into language, form, images, stories, ideas, explanations—everything, so that you can comprehend this and be able to relate to it within your own circumstances in life.

Fundamentally, there must be a completely new understanding and education regarding this. Some people believe that many of God's angels have fallen, have been seduced by the pleasures and the seductions of physical life and have fallen and become demons and that God is opposed by whole leagues of angels, or other beings who are opposed to God's reality.

This is certainly convenient because it identifies the opposition, but really the opposition is part of the reality of living life in Separation— the desire to be separate, the fear of giving up this Separation, the emphasis on one's uniqueness and all of the particulars of one's identity and psychology. People place great emphasis on what makes them unique, what gives them status, what gives them recognition and what makes them powerful or desirable.

This is the power that opposes the reality of life. Certainly, there are beings that are committed to this. There are even beings beyond your visible range who are committed to this. There are angels who are committed to this. But do not think that there is one fallen angel that is the source of all evil in this world or the whole universe. That is projecting an incorrect understanding.

It is a condition of living a life in Separation. People want to return to union with God, but they do not want to give up their separate life here. Nor should they. God never asks you to do that. For God gives you a greater purpose for being in the world. Instead of seeking escape and trying to fulfill yourself through your ambitions and ideas, God through Knowledge is giving you a greater purpose in the world.

That is how God redeems you—by giving you something really important to do with your life. God does not cast a spell over you, dissolving all of your anger, resentment, frustration and confusion of mind. For God did not create these things, so God cannot uncreate them.

Yet what God does through the Angelic Presence, and through Knowledge within you, is to give you something important to do in life. In fact, you were sent into this world to do certain specific things with certain specific people. It is unlikely that you have found this purpose or these people yet, but your heart yearns for them. Everything in your deeper nature is trying to take you to this purpose, and to these people, and to these forms of service to humanity and to the world.

The fact that people are neglecting this or avoiding this or denying this is the source of so much of their suffering. For without this greater purpose, without the relationships that serve this purpose, without the fulfillment of this purpose, no matter what you can do, no matter what you try to do, never satisfies the need of the soul.

For at the core of you is what God created in you, not what you created or what your society has created. Even the most dreadful or violent person in the world has at the center of them what God has created. Their ignorance, their rebellion, is the source of their frustration, ignorance and violence upon the world.

That is why God did not create Hell and does not punish the wicked. You want to punish the wicked to take out your revenge, to exact your notions of justice. But for God, there is only redemption of those who have fallen or who are lost. Individuals who live violent or destructive lives will have a much longer journey to take and will have to perform a far greater service to humanity to redeem themselves. But in the end, redemption is really what it is all about.

What is redemption? For you living in this world, in this life, at this time, redemption is discovering your greater purpose in the world— expressing it, accepting it and fulfilling it to the best of your ability. That is redemption for you at this time, within this reality. Beyond this, your intellect cannot go.

God has given you a greater life and has placed the reality of this greater life in Knowledge within you. Knowledge within you is beyond the realm and the reach of your intellect. It is something you must experience deeply within yourself and learn to trust and learn to follow. This will challenge you who are still attached to your goals, to your idea of yourself, to your condemnation of others and to all those things that have made up your separate reality. You will be challenged to follow Knowledge, for it is taking you in a different direction.

Whether you are religious or not, whether you believe in a religious teaching and adhere to that teaching, or whether you claim to have no religious affiliation, your progress is entirely dependent upon your connection to Knowledge.

There are individuals who lead major religious institutions who have no awareness of Knowledge and do not value it and perhaps even fear it, thinking that it would lead them into chaos, or that it would defy their religious beliefs or lead them into grave doubt and uncertainty. So they will cling to their ideas and their beliefs and avoid the power of redemption that God has placed within them.

Then there are people who will claim no religious affiliation, but who will experience and follow the power of Knowledge. They will have a chance to really redeem themselves through great service to others and to the world.

Whether you are religious or not is not the emphasis here. Religion can be very helpful if it is understood correctly, if it is seen as a pathway to Knowledge. But if it is held simply as a network of beliefs and social obligations, then it is moving in the wrong direction.

The Angelic Presence understands all this. God is watching over the entire universe. Not only is God watching over the entire universe,

God is watching over all of Creation that is not living in Separation, which is even greater than the physical manifestations of life and reality.

You walk down to the ocean with a little cup in your hand, and you dip it in the water and you look at the water. Is that water the ocean? Yes and no. Yes, it is part of the ocean, but is it the ocean? People try to claim the reality of God and the intention of God. People are even so arrogant as to think that God will not send another Messenger into the world, thinking that all of the Messages have been sent, and no more are really needed. They take their cup to the ocean, and they fill it, and they walk away thinking that they have the ocean. But they only have a tiny, tiny little bit—so tiny that it does not give the reality of the ocean, and all of the life that lives within the ocean.

So you take, instead of a cup, a bucket down to the ocean, and you fill it full of the ocean water. And now you think you understand God. You look in the bucket and you say, "Oh, this is the ocean. This is God." But God is so much greater, and your little bucket of water does not represent the diversity of life living within that ocean.

Using this as an analogy, if you try to claim the reality of God and God's purpose and intentions for the world, and you say, "This is it! This is God! This is what God wills for humanity! This is what God has given to humanity! This is the ultimate!" then it is like calling the bucket of water the entire ocean.

The ocean is vast. The universe is vast. It is full of life, beyond human estimation. The universe is like an ocean without end, the product of evolutionary forces that God has set in motion, at the beginning of the physical universe.

God does not have to manage your life. The mechanism of evolutionary change, and all of the biological and geological forces in your world, are creating the environment for your life. But God has placed Knowledge within you to guide you, to protect you and to lead you to your greater fulfillment and redemption.

Therefore, do not blame God for the hurricanes or the droughts or the pestilence or the pandemic illness or personal failure. People go around all day long saying, "Well, God is teaching me a lesson through this," as if God is their tutor, as if God is their handmaiden, as if God is the co-pilot of their life.

What kind of God is this? You are not talking about God now. You are talking about the Angelic Presence. All of the great Revelations to humanity have been given by the Angelic Presence. They speak as We not as I. They are a group and not just a magnificent individual.

There is so much to unlearn here. Humanity is still a primitive race in this regard, still believing in local deities and fantastic things. It is still very superstitious, still very self-preoccupied, still believing that it is significant and pre-eminent in the universe. But it is okay because that is just where you are in life.

You are like a 13-year-old. Humanity is like a 13-year-old beginning to experience some power, beginning to feel strong, beginning to want to expand and to express itself as a whole. But it is still immature. It is unaccountable and irresponsible. It does not really understand the requirements of life on a long-term scale. It has not emerged into a mature state where it must focus on stability and security more than growth and expansion.

That is the stage humanity is in. There are individuals who are far beyond this stage, of course. But, as a whole, humanity is in sort of the latter stages of its adolescence. It does not think ahead. It does not plan for the future. It does not use its resources wisely. It makes wild and foolish decisions. It is prone to fight amongst its members. It believes in the use of force. It is aggressive. It is violent. It is adolescent.

In the universe around you, there are much more mature races, at least mature in the sense that they value stability and security more than growth and expansion. But the discovery of Knowledge is rare even in the universe. And that is why the Angelic Presence that serves each world and each group is at work trying and working on bringing people to the reality of Knowledge within themselves. Regardless of their culture, their appearance, their belief systems, their traditions or the nature of oppression within their own societies, this is still the case because this is the Great Attraction of God.

God is not local. God does not show up and deliver a message to a group of people. That is always done through the Angelic Presence. Your encounter with God will be through the Angelic Presence and through the experience of Knowledge within yourself.

How do you know God? You begin to listen and to explore the deeper current of your life. You begin to take the Steps to Knowledge, which lead you, as if you were going down a spiral staircase, into a deeper well of intelligence that God has placed within you.

Your mind and imagination are floating above the surface like clouds, but down on the ground there is a deeper intelligence. It is solid. It is real. It is permanent. It has greater strength. It is certain. It does not vacillate from day to day, like your intellect or emotions. It is not prone to persuasion and denial, like your intellect and emotions.

God does not want you to lose yourself in God, in some kind of ecstasy. Rather, you are sent here to perform certain services to others and with others, specific things in the world. That is why you have a unique nature and a unique design. But if you do not know what your nature is for, or what you were designed to do, then you will tend to misconstrue yourself and compare yourself with others whom you think are more impressive. But you are truly designed for something you have not yet discovered.

So it is the discovery of this purpose that begins to bring clarity to your life. You begin to accept and understand yourself—your strengths and your weaknesses. You are designed for something unique. What is that? Your intellect does not know; your culture does not know; your family probably does not know. That is why taking the Steps to Knowledge is the essential thing. That is why at the core of all the world's religions, there is the pathway to Knowledge. Perhaps these pathways exist in the mystical traditions, but they are pathways nonetheless.

God has sent a New Message into the world to prepare humanity for the Great Waves of change that are coming to the world, and for humanity's encounter with the Greater Community of intelligent life in the universe.

God's New Message has also been sent to provide another pathway to Knowledge, a pathway that has not been corrupted and misused by political powers or by social forces. It is a pure pathway. It is not the only pathway, certainly, but it is a new pathway to redefine and to clarify the nature of God's functioning in the world, God's Plan and the Divine nature of all individuals.

The New Message from God represents the preparation for a whole new era of human experience—an era that will be fraught with great environmental difficulties and great political and economic instability, an era in which humanity will have to face the difficulties of emerging into a Greater Community of intelligent life, an era where humanity will have to choose whether to unite and to succeed or whether to contend with itself and to fail. This has required a new Revelation from the Creator of all life.

You are fortunate to be able to learn of this. This Teaching you are hearing and reading at this moment is part of that New Revelation. It is a process of clarification to dispel layers and layers of confusion and misinterpretation, to give you clarity and strength and purpose and to bring you to Knowledge within yourself—your deeper conscience, your deeper intelligence.

This is where God's Will moves you and restrains you, takes you here and not there, directs you to unite with this person and not with these other people. It is what gives you the strength to know which way to go at every turn of the road, how to respond to each new event in life and how to ride the growing waves of uncertainty and instability in a world undergoing profound change.

Here there are no heroes, and there is no person to worship. There are great individuals and great emissaries of course, but only God is God. Everything else is the Creation.

Then there is fantasy. You live in a world where fantasy has to compete with reality, where even reality is not clearly understood. So it is a very confusing situation. God understands this, and that is why the Angelic Presence oversees the world and is available to assist you when you earnestly desire assistance.

The Angelic Presence may not give you what you request, but it will bring you closer to Knowledge, which is such a greater answer.

If you simply ask for favors without realizing that you are lost, you are really asking for so little. It is Knowledge within you that will enable you to regain your awareness of who you are and why you are here, where you must go and what you must do. This sense of determination will be natural to you, and it will give you a sense of freedom and liberation.

Finally, you can be who you are, and do what you came here to do, and be free to choose what is really right for you instead of being bound by other obligations, cast under a yoke of other requirements, chained to a wall of your social obligations. For your first responsibility is to Knowledge because that is your responsibility to God.

The Angelic Presence that oversees this world understands the human condition and the whole history of the human condition. They are focused upon that. They are like translators, trying to translate a greater reality into this reality so that human beings can become powerful and inspired and provide great service to the benefit of humanity and to the world.

This enables you to be redeemed here and to take on a greater responsibility and level of service in the universe. This is beyond your awareness and is beyond your focus for now, for it is this life that must be a success. And what makes it a success is not fulfilling the expectations of society, but fulfilling the greater purpose that God has given you to experience, to express and to contribute in the world, as it is today, and to do this without condemnation and without self-hatred or hatred for others.

This is who you are and why you are here. And the journey before you is immense. And it is fundamental to your well-being, your fulfillment and your success. It is mysterious because it transcends human understanding and human preoccupation. And yet it is so fundamental and natural to you that you will instantly recognize its value once you experience it. It is natural for you because it represents your deeper nature and your deeper purpose.

Everywhere in the universe God redeems the separated through Knowledge. And the Angelic Presence that serves all worlds is part of the Plan to bring this awareness to those who are separated, to encourage freedom, creativity, honesty and compassion.

This is a universal teaching. It is going on everywhere. Everywhere in the universe, there is a struggle between oppression and freedom, between ignorance and wisdom. It is a battle that goes on in the minds and hearts of people everywhere—not only in this world, but everywhere.

Of course, this is challenging. Of course, it will require a re-evaluation. Of course, it is upsetting to certain people's beliefs and expectations. Even longstanding traditions will have to be reconsidered in light of this. But that is healthy for humanity. It is healthy that you have clarification, that you reconsider your values, your beliefs and your ideas. That is what creates progress. That is what can open your life to the redeeming power and presence that God has placed within you.

CHAPTER 10

HOW GOD SPEAKS TO THE WORLD

*As revealed to
Marshall Vian Summers
on April 16, 2008
in Tehran, Iran*

God watches over the world, for the world is a troubled place. It has always been so.

That is why you have come to the world. It is a place where God has been forgotten, and your true nature has been forgotten. It is a place of competition and conflict, where life is difficult, where you must constantly solve the problems of your daily existence. It is a place where people seem foreign to one another and foreign to themselves as God has created them. It is a place of appearances. It is a place of sensations.

It is wonderful and dangerous, beautiful, but confusing. It is where the separated have come to live, to learn how to give again and to bridge the gap so that the Separation may be ended in time.

No one has come here by accident. Everyone has been sent for a purpose. This purpose remains undiscovered within you, but you must find it, for that is the great pursuit in life. Beyond meeting your basic requirements to exist in this reality, you must find this purpose, for this is how God will speak to you, and this is how you will find your way.

115

The Plan of God is so very simple that it escapes people's comprehension, yet it is mysterious because it does not fit in with human expectations. It does not fit in with human beliefs and traditions. It is beyond comprehension, and yet it is very simple.

For God speaks to the world through a deeper Knowledge within the individual and through the power of united relationships, where this deeper power can be expressed and experienced between two or more people.

Periodically, God speaks to the world to deliver a Message to the world. This is very infrequent, perhaps only happening every few centuries. God's Message to the world is meant to last for a very long time and is meant to affect and influence the minds and hearts of people for a very long time. These Messages are given at pivotal points in human evolution and at great times of change and times of great need.

The meaning of this is beyond your current references, for you do not see yet the great need of humanity and why a New Message from God would be sent into the world, for the world itself. For while God speaks to you through a deeper Knowledge within yourself and through the power of united relationships, God's Message to the world is to prepare humanity for what it cannot see and cannot know. It is to warn humanity. It is to empower humanity. It is to prepare humanity.

You can only be a witness to this. It will be beyond your current ideas. It will transcend your understanding. But God is not trying to reach your intellect as much as to resonate within you at a deeper level. For the intellect was created to navigate and to comprehend physical things, particular things. But the deeper resonance is of the soul, and that is how you will respond to God's great, but infrequent, Messages for humanity.

People have many questions, but they must learn to listen at a deeper level, to still their minds and to listen, to be present, to be observant, to be reverent.

For the intellect cannot know for sure if a New Message from God is authentic. They [people] cannot know for sure if what they are hearing is absolutely the truth, the greater truth from the Creator of all life. They cannot know with their intellect if the Messenger is the real Messenger. But in their heart they will know. The resonance will be deeper. The recognition will emerge from a deeper awareness within you and within others.

This is what has kept religion alive. It is this deeper resonance. It is not the power of belief, for belief is weak and fallible and is easily manipulated by others, by other powers and forces and so forth. But the resonance that keeps people responding to God's great Messages is happening at a deeper level within the individual—beyond their intellect, beyond their ideas and comprehension—and this is what gives it power and magnificence.

But if you cannot respond at this deeper level, then it becomes a matter of ideology, of belief and of social and political adherence. It becomes a matter of conformity and the expectations of others. You are expected to believe, so you believe. You are expected to pray, so you pray. You are expected to follow the requirements that have been set down before, mostly by human beings, of course. But God speaks to you at a deeper level.

God speaks to the world through these great Messages. They are beyond the immediate needs of the individual. They encompass the needs of humanity as a whole and are for the welfare and evolution of humanity as a whole.

From this, you gain a sense of your place and purpose in life at this time—why you are here at this time, in this place, in your particular circumstances, in your nation.

You must have this greater perspective. Otherwise, you will not understand the larger context in which your life exists, and you will not understand the movement of the world or the signs of the world. You will think it all a reference to the past—that in some way the present and the future are a fulfillment of the past. Ideas are associated with the past, but the deeper Knowledge that God has placed within you is for the present, the moment and for the future. So very different this is as an understanding.

God is not concerned if you have religion or not. But God is calling to you at this deeper level through the great Message for the world that is now being given to the world and through the power and influence of Knowledge within yourself. And that happens every day, every moment, in every year, at every time and in every place.

Even if you read the scriptures and they move you deeply, that is because of the resonance, not because of the ideas. The Power of God is not limited by human understanding, or human ideas, or the ideas of any race in the universe, of which there are so very many.

God is speaking now to the world through the New Message from God and through the Messenger that has been sent to the world to prepare humanity to face a world in decline—a world whose resources are diminishing; a world where people will have to cooperate with one another and end their ceaseless conflicts; a world that is entering a dangerous period, more dangerous than any period you have ever known; a world that is facing contact with life in the universe; a world that is facing intervention from races from the universe who are here to take advantage of a weak and divided humanity.

The human family as a whole has never had to face these two great challenges—living in a world in decline and facing competition from beyond the world for who will control the world and who will be pre-eminent here. The great Messages that God has sent into the world [before] cannot prepare you for this. That is why there is a New Message from God.

Never think that God has stopped communicating to the world. Never think that the final Message for all time has been given. This is human presumption. This is established to protect a belief and an ideology.

But God watches over the world. And humanity is now facing its greatest challenges as a whole. How will it respond? How will it prepare? Will it be able to comprehend the great change that is coming? Will it fight and struggle with itself over the remaining resources? Will it unite to defend the world against foreign intervention? This is a time of great decision: whether humanity will fail or whether humanity will unite for its preservation and to preserve its sovereignty in this world.

You see right away here how far beyond your own personal preoccupations this is—beyond your daily concerns, beyond your ideas, beyond your beliefs, beyond your religious understanding, beyond your political views, beyond the need of the day. If you are only consumed with the needs of the day, how will you see the Great Waves of change that are coming that will alter the landscape? How will you read the signs of the world that speak of greater things beyond your own personal concerns? How will you know when something is about to change your life? Will you be standing on the shore when the Great Waves come, your back to the sea—not watching, not looking, not listening?

That is why God's great Messages transcend the understanding and the awareness of the people at the time that the great Messages are given. You will have to have a much greater perspective and be much higher on the mountain to see the relevance and importance of this.

People will think God's New Message is irrelevant. It is impossible. It will seem to not meet their daily concerns. They will not see that it is here to save humanity itself. They will not see what it really is. So it will be neglected and avoided, criticized and ridiculed.

People want bread for today. They do not see that when God speaks to the entire world, it is for the preservation of the entire world. It is for the preservation of humanity. Without this, there will not be bread for anyone in the future. That is why the New Message has been given.

You must become still and listen with your heart here. Your ideas will be struggling. They will be struggling to keep up. They will be trying to calculate and comprehend this. But they cannot, you see, for this is not a Message for the intellect.

This is speaking to a deeper intelligence within you, an intelligence not created by the world, but created by God to guide you, to protect you and to enable you to respond.

Forget your ideas of religion now, for you are facing a New Message from God. Forget the precepts from the past, for this is for the present and the future.

This is to determine if humanity will have a future, a future that you could possibly desire and embrace. This is for the protection of humanity, everyone here, living in a world in decline, living in a world that is facing intervention from beyond and competition from beyond.

You must see the connection. If you do not think this is important for you, then you have lost contact with life. You do not see what provides for humanity.

God has provided this abundant world for the human family. If it is despoiled, if it is ruined, if it is depleted, God is not going to create another world for you. You are going to have to live with the consequences.

If your resources are not managed and shared and preserved when necessary, do you think God is going to come and bring you a new world—you just pack up and move to another planet somewhere? What is your thinking here? Do you think you are alone in the universe and no one is aware of you, that others do not desire this place for themselves?

This is beyond the current concerns of people—their daily focus, their work, their ideology, their beliefs, their religion and their political ideas. Governments are not meeting to discuss how humanity is going to survive within a Greater Community of intelligent life. It is not part of the public debate or conversation. People are not talking about this in the café.

That is why there is a New Message from God, and that is why you must listen now because this has everything to do with your world, your future, who you are as an individual and why you were sent into the world in the first place.

It is this Knowledge that God has placed within you that will enable you to hear and to respond. If you are not connected to this Knowledge, then it will all seem like foreign ideas to you. But if you can listen with the heart, you will see and know that this is the great Message for your time and for the times to come.

God will not give another Message to humanity for a long time to come. This is it. If you cannot hear, it is a great misfortune for you. This is it. There is no Message around the corner. There is no second version. There is no Message that is going to come and be what you want it to be.

This is it. This is the Voice of the New Message. It is a Voice like this that has delivered the Messages throughout human history.

You wonder at my language. I represent all the languages in one language. But I speak through this language [English] to you because this is the most universal language in the world today. It has the greatest reach, the greatest possibility. My accent is all accents.

It is not important that you try to comprehend these things, but it is important that you listen, that you receive God's New Message—not fight with it, not contend with it, not argue with it, not think you have to believe in it, but to listen, to stop your ceaseless grasping thoughts and listen. You will only know if this is true by a deeper resonance within yourself. The challenge is upon you, you see.

All the great Messengers have been denied and ridiculed, persecuted and even killed because people could not hear. They could not feel.

It is the same problem today. You have a modern society, a modern technology, but the same problem exists. It is the problem of living in Separation. It is the problem of being dominated by your mind, your thoughts and your beliefs. It is the problem of a lack of human freedom in your societies. People are under the weight of survival and governments. Even religions become oppressive. But it is the same problem. It has always been the same problem. So the Messenger is denied, disbelieved, suspected, criticized, condemned, ignored or avoided. It is the same problem.

What will it take for you to realize you are living at a time of Revelation? It is in this time that a New Message from God has come into the world. Will you stand around shaking your head? Will you run away? You see, it is the same problem.

How will you know? You will know because God has put the power of Knowledge within you, far beneath and beyond your ideas, your concepts, your admonitions and your traditions.

God is speaking to the world now. You must listen for what God has to say to the world. Stop talking. Stop thinking. Stop debating. Stop resisting. And listen. If you do not listen, you will not even know what you are responding to.

Humanity's two great challenges will determine the fate and the future of everyone in the world, the fate and future of all the nations, of the peoples, the condition of the world itself and whether humanity will be able to maintain its sovereignty in this world.

You have lived so long in isolation, you think that you are alone in the vastness of space. But the universe is full of life. You live on a beautiful planet. There are races who are aware of it, that seek it for themselves. How will you defend it? How will you preserve it? How will you protect it? How will you maintain humanity's ability to survive here?

To do this, you must become a united humanity. Your nations must cooperate. You must end your ceaseless conflicts. You must see this is born of necessity now. It is not merely an ideal or a wish. It is a necessity.

God is speaking to the world. This is how God speaks to the world. This is how simple it is, how pure it is. It is not sensational. It does not fit people's expectations. It is not here as a confirmation of people's ideas or expectations. This is how God speaks to the world.

The New Message is very great. It has taken a long time to present it here. The Messenger is in the world. You must hear the Message. You must listen with your heart. You must allow God to reveal to you the state of the world, the future of humanity and the great decisions before governments, people, individuals and you as to how you will live, what you will choose, your comprehension of where humanity is going and the great challenges before you now. God provides what humanity cannot see and cannot know for the next great step in your long history here.

CHAPTER 11

GOD'S PLAN IS TO SAVE EVERYONE

As revealed to
Marshall Vian Summers
on October 14, 2014
in Boulder, Colorado

Today We shall speak of God's Great Love for the world.

Living in Separation, people have chosen to come into a world of
difficulty, a world of change, a world requiring constant adaptation,
a world of competition for resources, a world of beauty, but a world
of adversity as well. This is the natural world, which you may admire,
but within which you must learn to survive. It is not an easy task.

Heaven has created this environment throughout the universe as
a place for the separated to live, for those who chose to come into
form and to be individualized in this way. It is an environment of
growth and expansion, an environment that few in this world
really understand.

Choosing Separation, you had to come into a very different
environment from that which you have left. And different it is, truly.
You cannot imagine your Ancient Home, living in Separation. And
indeed it is difficult to imagine living in a physical environment when
you are dwelling in your Ancient Home, which you will return
to eventually.

For God's Plan is to save everyone. It is a Plan so exquisite, so perfect,
you can hardly imagine it—a Plan not only for the human family,

for this one little world alone, but for the entire universe and the universes beyond it and all the dimensions of physical existence and manifestation.

That is why the ancient religions cannot really give you the complete picture, for they do not speak of life beyond this world. But what God is doing beyond this world is what God is doing here.

So for the first time in history, the great understanding is being given to the human family as you stand at the threshold of space, as you stand at the threshold of encountering intelligent life in the universe—intelligent life which is already in the world.

For the first time in history, you are being given a greater panorama of life in which to understand yourself, your life and your purpose for being in the world at this time. But to see this and to understand this, you must have a greater understanding and comprehension, not bound in ancient philosophies and theology, but bound in a greater understanding of God's Work in the universe.

For the first time in all of history, this is being given to the human family, not as a grand journey for a few people to take and to experience, but for the safety of humanity, the preservation of human civilization and the cultivation of a greater freedom in the world, greater than anything that has been established here before.

The purpose then is of critical importance. Do not think this is a personal journey of excitement. It is a blueprint for survival in a Greater Community of life in the universe. It is a blueprint for uniting the world's religions sufficiently that they will cease their opposition to one another and begin to support one another, each giving unique features, practices and understanding to the human family. For God has initiated them all, and they are all here to serve the growth and preservation of the human family.

But you cannot see this yet, for you are mired in conflict and controversy. You are mired in judgment and condemnation. You are mired in partisanship and opposition to others. Your notion of God is singularly lacking in this regard.

God is the Source of all the world's religions, and yet they fight one another vehemently and have for centuries indeed. Standing at the threshold of a Greater Community of life, you cannot afford this destructive and tragic activity any longer.

God knows what humanity must have. God knows what is coming over the horizon. God does not want to see humanity fail as it destroys its foundation in the world and as it faces, unprepared, a universe, a competitive environment greater than anything you can see here on Earth.

This is the Love of God. You are free to be living in Separation, for you were made to be free. You are even free to leave your Ancient Home. You are free to live in Separation, but your connection with God has never ceased.

Part of your mind is still connected to God. Part of your mind can respond to God's Guidance, Power and Presence. Part of your mind, beyond the realm and the reach of the intellect, is still connected to your Ancient Home and to all of Creation that exist beyond the physical realm.

Do not think this is too big for you to understand, for this is your natural state We speak of here today. It has everything to do with why you are in the world, whom you must meet, what you must do and what you must avoid if you are to play your part in God's Greater Plan for humanity and for all life in the universe.

God is far greater than any religion has ever conceived or could conceive, in this world or any world—a God of a billion, billion, billion races and more, a God of galaxies beyond this one, a God of Creation beyond all physical manifestation. No theology or philosophy could contain this panorama of life, wisdom, power and intention.

So understand that all your religious beliefs are relative in nature, relative to time, space and change. They are all an approximation.

If they are understood correctly, they will assist you in moving forward. They will assist you in organizing your life and in living correctly so you do not generate shame and unworthiness for yourself.

But religion is not conceived correctly. The Love of God is now clothed in petitions for miracles and dispensations. And God is still portrayed as angry, vengeful and punishing at the core of most of the world's theologies.

Therefore, to understand the Love of God, to understand God's Plan to save everyone, you must have the eyes to see beyond what you are accustomed to, beyond perhaps what you have been taught. Beyond your religious and social conditioning, to a certain degree, you must see.

And when you do, the meaning of your life will begin to become apparent. You will feel as if you have been freed from a prison, a prison within your own mind, a prison of conditioning and religious belief.

For you do not get to Heaven based upon belief. Your road to Heaven has to do with contribution in the world, based upon tolerance, forgiveness and service to others. Be you of any faith tradition, be you of no faith tradition, your life is either purposeful in this regard or not. Bowing down to God means nothing if you will not follow what God has given you to follow within yourself.

For God is not bound by the scriptures, and what God has put within you is beyond the scriptures. Let the scriptures prepare you for this deeper engagement, but let them not replace this deeper engagement.

For part of you is still connected to God, and that is the part you must learn to recognize, to discern amongst the other voices and impulses in your mind, the part that you must learn to follow, the part you hold in common with all others who dwell here.

Everyone is in the world for a purpose, but only this part of you knows what that is and is bound to guide you, if possible, to meet your rendezvous with others, and to prepare you for a greater life of service and fulfillment here.

All that We are telling you here today will prepare you for understanding God's Plan to save everyone.

God is not shocked by your errors. God is not shocked by all of the tragedies of humanity here on Earth—its cruelty, its destruction. God is not shocked by your errors, your foolishness, your self-deprecation, your deprecation of others because God knows that without this Knowledge to guide you, you will live in confusion, and from confusion will come error, and from error will come cruelty and violence towards yourself and others.

God will not punish you for this, for God knows that if you are not connected to the deeper Knowledge that God has put within you, the part of you that has never left God, your errors will be inevitable. Even if you try to live a very good and upright life, you will still be confused and constantly hounded by your uncertainty and misery, and in judgment of the world around you.

People try to adapt to this in every conceivable way, either positively or negatively, but it all ends up being really the same. For without Knowledge, you do not know where you have come from. You do not know what you are doing. You do not know where you really need to go in life. And all the while you feel an emptiness inside, recognizing, at least momentarily here and there, that you are not living the life you are meant to live.

Even if you have wealth and splendor, even if you seem to have everything that society garners as valuable, this emptiness will still reside within you unless you are following that which you must follow, which is beyond comprehension, but which is the most powerful experience you can have in life, once you begin this engagement.

God knows you could not separate completely from Heaven and Creation. And in your journey here in physical reality, you would lose sight of it because it is so very difficult to live in this environment.

Your natural state, your natural resonance with Creation, would be replaced by all of the impressions of the world; by the pain of the world; by the follies of the world; by the inducements of others, forcing you to adapt, very unnaturally often, to your circumstances, to your family, to your culture, to your religion until you become so distorted that you have no notion of yourself. You are a stranger to yourself. You judge yourself as you judge all others, based upon impressions and values that have been inculcated in you by your culture, that are not native to who you are.

God understands these things. God has put Knowledge within you to guide you, to protect you and to lead you to a greater life of service in the world.

But this requires a new approach. While The Way of Knowledge has been part of every world religion, it has been held back, so the people of the world could not have it, could not find it, could not hear of it. Held back, by ruling powers. Held back, by ecclesiastical bodies. Held back, by rulers of nations.

This kind of freedom was unknown in the ancient world except in very rare exceptions and is unknown today in large parts of the world. That people could be inner directed seems like a threat to society, to governance, to stability, to culture.

But if you could understand what We are saying today, you would understand that Knowledge within you cannot be in opposition to Knowledge within another. And this is the great peacemaker in the world.

You may make peace agreements. You may hold back the aggression of war. You may restrain nations and peoples from attacking each other, but you have not yet achieved what will really be required to establish an equitable and just society here.

God has put a deeper conscience within all people. If this is overlaid, they will not experience it, except perhaps here and there, in moments of fear or guilt or confusion.

The part of you that never left God is just. It is not in opposition to others. Viewpoints will differ. Approaches will differ. Understanding will not be the same in this world. But Knowledge can override all of these things between people of different nations, different religions, different cultures, different orientations. All these things that stand between people, that separate people, that cast people in conflict with each other can be overridden by what We speak of here today.

For God's Plan is to save everyone. But God's Plan is not what people think or understand. This will take time, but time is nothing to God. Time is everything to you, who live in time and must concern yourself with not wasting time—the time of your life, the value of your life, the time that you have been given here.

God's Plan is to save everyone. This will change the religious beliefs and philosophies of the world's religions. But it must be given with a whole New Message from God, for it is not simply an idea alone. It is creating a whole new understanding, an understanding that is native to who you are, that applies to everyone, that applies to other races in the universe, that applies to the whole universe. For God does not have a different Plan for every single little world.

The God We speak of is so vast, and yet God speaks to you in the most intimate part of you—a place sacred, a place eternal, a place so deep. You must go to this depth if you are to understand and have the authentic experience of engagement that We speak of here today.

God's Plan is to reclaim all the separated everywhere, for you can never really be apart from God completely. So even if you create Hell on Earth for yourself and others, you are still connected to God.

Knowledge is with you—here, there and everywhere. You can never lose it. It can never be taken from you. You can forget it. You can deny it. You can run away from it. You can live a life apart from it. But it is always with you.

You are tethered to Heaven, you see. No matter how degrading your life in the world, no matter how brutal your circumstances, no matter how terrible the political or religious oppression under which you live, you are still connected in this way, and this is how God will save you.

God does not care about your religious beliefs. Their value is only to the degree to which they can connect you with this deeper intelligence, this deeper part of you that We speak of.

Having a wonderful or correct belief will not bridge the gap between you and your Source. Believing in one teacher will not make a difference here. Believing in one of the great Messengers who has come to the Earth from the Angelic Assembly is not enough.

You must follow that which was given you to follow. You must live your life according to this, within religion or beyond religion, wherever you are destined to be. This is how God will save you.

When you have completed your learning here in the world, you will join a greater Assembly that oversees life in this world to help those who remain behind. Your accomplishments will not be wasted.

When you no longer need to be in this world or live in physical reality, your training is still not yet complete. You will enter a level of service to assist those who remain behind. This is how God puts everyone living in Separation to work for the salvation of all. A Plan so beautiful you cannot even imagine how it works. A Plan so complete that it cannot fail in time.

But time is your problem, you see, for you are languishing in time. You are suffering in time. Your life is being misspent. You are not going anywhere. You are not finding that which you must find and doing that which you must do. Not yet. Perhaps you are close. Perhaps you are far away.

This is the Calling of Heaven. This is how God will save everyone. To accept this, you must learn to have regard for yourself and others. You must see your errors are the result of living without Knowledge. You must see that the tragedies, the errors and the conflicts of humanity are all the results of people not being aware of these things We speak of.

Without Knowledge, people will identify with their ideas and their beliefs, their political agenda, their religious agenda, much of which is based upon conflict and opposition to others.

It is a hopeless situation. But there is a way out of this jungle, and God has put the power within you to lead you out, step by step. You will not understand as you proceed. You need only take the next step. You do not understand yet what is really happening in your life. But you must trust yourself enough, and you must stop condemning others so that your mind can open, so that you can begin to respond.

God's New Revelation in the world is calling out to the whole world and providing the pathway that is at the heart of all the world's religions, but that has never been made available before.

For God's Plan is to save everyone. And your being in the world is part of this Plan.

CHAPTER 12

THE HEART OF GOD

*As revealed to
Marshall Vian Summers
on January 25, 2015
in Jerusalem, Israel*

To know the Heart of God, you must understand how God works in the world, and how God views those who live in Separation and are circumscribed in Separation living in the physical reality. For part of Creation has entered the physical universe to experience Separation by their own choice.

Living here, however, is a difficult situation. It leads people into confusion, where they forget their Ancient Home and their Source and those who watch over them. God knows living in Separation people will be confused. They will fall under the persuasions of the world. They will fall under the persuasions of their cultures and societies, and even religion itself, as it has been formulated here on Earth.

God knows without the deeper Knowledge that God has placed within each person—a beacon to help them to return Homeward—without this, all manner of confusion, conflict and evil can arise. And such has been the case here on Earth.

But God loves Creation. And Creation loves God. And though you are living in Separation, in the physical reality, though you appear to be an individual separated from other individuals, separated from your Source, and within yourself separated from the deeper

Knowledge that God has placed there, you are still part of Creation. God still loves you. And you love God.

You can never lose this. Even if you live the most depraved and sinful life, you never lose this.

That is why it is the source of your redemption. God's Love for you and your love for God are what redeem you. The Knowledge that God has placed within you holds this love, makes this connection and keeps it alive forever and ever. Even if you live in the farthest reaches of Separation, it holds your connection to God and to the Heart of God, which is connected to your heart and soul.

In this, there can be no condemnation. There is no Judgment Day, as people think of it, as it has been taught and reinforced in this world. There is no Hell and damnation. But there is the Hell of Separation, and you are living in that Hell now.

Be you rich or poor, you are separated from your Source. You are separated from those who watch over you from beyond the world, from beyond the physical reality. You are separated from Knowledge within yourself, which represents the part of you that has never left God.

Your soul is adrift in the universe, adrift on a great ocean, lost. But because God has put Knowledge within you, God knows where you are. And when you are ready, God will call you to begin to return.

Once you grow tired of seeking fulfillment here, once you become discouraged by your own ambitions and the ambitions of others, once you realize you cannot fulfill yourself here living in Separation, once you realize you cannot replicate here on Earth what you had before you came, then you will reach a point, a turning point. And slowly, incrementally, you will begin your return.

God knows you will return eventually, but in time you languish and suffer, and suffer the cruelty of others, and your own harshness towards yourself. You suffer from so many things. You cannot relieve this suffering except by beginning the return, by reconnecting with the Knowledge that God has placed within you, which holds for you your redemption.

Knowledge is not here to take you out of the world but to bring you here with a greater purpose. For God has given you a greater purpose for being here, in this world, under the very circumstances that you tend to avoid or deny, under the reality of your situation.

God seeks to put you to work in your own unique way, playing your part, to undo Separation within yourself and between yourself and others. And you will continue this work beyond this life. For when you leave here, you do not go to Heaven or Hell. You enter another level of service, serving those who remain behind, assisting them when you can, watching over them.

It is a perfect Plan. It is God's Greater Plan that no religion in this world or any world could ever contain. How could your religious understanding account for a universe of a billion, billion, billion races and more, in this galaxy and other galaxies, all living in Separation? And even the immense expanse of the physical reality is but a small part of God's timeless Creation.

It is only as you undo Separation that you will begin to understand what caused Separation. Right now you cannot understand this. Your religions cannot understand this. The smartest person in the world cannot understand this, for they are still circumscribed by Separation.

That is why there are no masters living in the world, for mastery is beyond the world. Though there are those who are wise and competent and have vision, mastery is beyond this world—at a higher level, beyond the fog of the world, beyond the clouds of confusion here, here on the ground, you see.

That is why your religions can only be approximations of a greater truth. Living in time and space and change, you can only see a part. That is why God has given the great Revelations to the world, to begin to be testaments to this Greater Reality. One great Revelation alone cannot do this completely. You actually need them all.

They represent God's great care for this world, and for other worlds that are far less free than you are at this moment. For freedom is rare in the universe. It is so difficult to achieve amongst the nations of the separated. But it can be achieved, and if it is, it is a great gift not only to that world and those people, but to the whole universe.

What We are telling you here today represents the Heart of God. For there is no malice in God. There is no revenge in God. There is no cruelty or punishment in God. Therefore, you cannot use religion as a banner of war or a legal principle to punish others, to torture others or to execute others. That is a crime against God and God's Will and Purpose for the world. Any scripture or interpretation that advocates these things is inauthentic and misunderstood.

Why would God punish you when God knows that without the Knowledge that God has placed within you to guide you that you would fall into error and conflict and would become cruel towards yourself and others? Why would God punish you when you are foolish and ignorant? God does forgive you because you do not know what you are doing.

Until Knowledge can guide you—the Knowledge that God has placed there, in every person, religious or not, in every culture and nation—until you can follow this, then you do not know what you are doing. You do not know your purpose. You do not know your destiny. You do not know who has sent you here and for what purpose. You are lost, afloat, adrift, languishing in time, trying to be happy, trying to avoid pain, falling into corruption in a corrupt world, full of corruption.

God knows without the blessings of Creation, you would lose all of the benefits of Creation. God knows that being separate from your Ancient Home, you would lose all of the benefits of your Ancient Home.

Hell and damnation is a human invention to corral people into believing, to threaten them. But the tragedy is that if you do not receive God's Revelations, the one that is meant for you, and do not learn to understand it, then you will languish in Separation, and you will be unable to escape it.

It is as if you had descended down into a deep ravine or canyon and God has sent down ladders to help you climb out. But if you do not climb out, you are still stuck there. You cannot wish yourself out. God is not going to just elevate you someday and erase all your errors. And belief will not bring you out because belief is not true yet unless it is guided by Knowledge.

You cannot believe your way out of this situation. You must learn to climb up the other side, using the ladders that God has dropped down. And God has dropped down more than one ladder because God knows that not everyone will follow one ladder alone. God knows that not everyone will follow one Teaching or Teacher alone. And God knows that every great Revelation brought to the world will be corrupted by people over time, and so there must be further Revelations to bring clarification and correction to all the errors that humanity has made with the previous Revelations.

It is the Love of God and the caring of God for you and for all who dwell here that give rise to this great offering of redemption.

God has a perfect Plan. It is beyond the ownership of any religion, but each religion can approximate it and aim you in the proper direction if it is free of condemnation, if it is free of the errors of humanity, who foolishly assume they know the Will of God and how God works in the world.

They think they understand the Mystery, but they have not even begun to understand the Mystery. The Mystery is what exists beyond your intellectual understanding. The pathway to God is beyond your intellectual understanding. You must be willing to go beyond if you are to continue in your return.

Those who become religious fundamentalists are locked in cages on the side of the mountain. They cannot proceed upward. They have built around them a wall, further separating them from those around them, deepening their Separation. Even while they espouse their religious principles, they are deepening their Separation, becoming further and further away from the Will and Purpose of God in the world.

That is why religious figures will tend to oppose a New Revelation in the world. It threatens their beliefs, the foundation upon which they have invested themselves. It challenges them to go beyond their ideas and their ideology because this is all of the mind and not of the heart and the soul. The soul returns to God without presumption, without admonition, without condemnation.

So God has initiated all the world's religions, each a critical building block in building human civilization on a higher ethical principle, keeping the power of Knowledge alive in the world, where it has died out or was never fostered in other nations in other worlds in the universe.

All the religions are important. They balance each other—the excesses and extremism of one another. They correct the errors of the past. They refine the approach because God knows that not everyone can follow one pathway or one Teacher, even the great Messengers.

So like the rivers all flowing to the same sea, they join and unite at a higher level. And though their ideology may differ and be in contrast to one another, it is all for a greater purpose.

For your return to God is not an intellectual enterprise. It is not built upon a mountain of belief and assumption. For true belief will lead you to the Mystery. And Mystery will take you beyond belief because God and Creation exist beyond human understanding, or the understanding of any race in the universe. For who can presume to know the God of all of Creation, of countless worlds like yours, of countless races so different from humanity?

For the first time in history, God is throwing open the doors to life in the universe and to God's greater Work in the universe. For to understand what God is doing in this world, you must understand what God is doing in the whole universe.

It was never possible before to present these things because humanity was still in a very primitive state. But humanity now stands at the threshold of space, and intervention from races from beyond the world has already begun—a dangerous intervention, a secret intervention. So humanity must learn of these things now, and only God's New Revelation can prepare you for this.

Humanity has also changed the world so sufficiently that it will now change on its own, producing a new world experience of great difficulty and hazard for the human family, a change on a level never seen before in the world. Therefore, God has spoken again to prepare you for this.

The religions of the world are contentious with each other and divided internally. And religious fundamentalism and religious violence are rising here and there with great destruction, further dividing the human family, further fracturing the human family, further weakening the human family at a time when human cooperation and unity are vital for your future in a declining world.

The Heart of God knows this and has sent a New Revelation to bring clarification, to restore your understanding of the purpose of all the world's religions and how each must now play a part in uniting humanity and preparing humanity for the Great Waves of change that are coming to this world and for its encounter with a universe full of intelligent life—the two greatest events in all of human history.

The religions of the world must now be part of the solution and not part of the problem, for they were meant to unite humanity and be a great asset to humanity. But this requires great clarification and restoration of their initial purpose and meaning and what Heaven wills for them now, which is being provided through the New Revelation from God because God knows without the New Revelation, humanity will continue to struggle, and as resources in the world decline and as populations grow, the prospect of endless war and destruction faces you.

God knows this, of course, and is attempting to rescue humanity from a condition that it has created for itself, a condition that many races in the universe have created, often leading to great tragedy.

It is because God loves you and you love God that this great Revelation has been given. It is for this reason that the past Revelations were given, given only once perhaps in a millennium, given for the moment and for the times to come, and to prepare humanity for a future it cannot even foresee—so great is the gift of each Revelation.

You know not of these things, not yet. But your comprehension must grow. You must grow beyond divisiveness and the discrimination and oppression of others. You must grow beyond the divisions of religion to understand the purpose of religion, and the Will of Heaven regarding religion.

God knows how to redeem you, one and all. Why do you presume you know what will redeem you? Your beliefs can only point you in the right direction. Beyond this, it is the power of Grace and the mysterious engagement with Knowledge within yourself and the purposeful engagement with the world that will restore to you your true direction, and what you are here to uniquely give to a world of increasing need and desperation.

You are here to give and to serve, not to criticize and condemn. You are here to forgive and build bridges to one another, not to burn them down and fight each other endlessly over your ideas, your preoccupations, your greed and your fear.

It is only a humanity that can cooperate between its nations and religions that will be able to prepare you for a declining world and will give you strength and efficacy in the universe, where you will be facing united worlds.

Human unity here is not just a good idea. It is not just a high moral principle. It is the requirement for survival in the universe if you are to be a free and self-determined race, contending now with powers that are not free.

You can do this, but it must require a great change of understanding, a great reckoning, a great facing of reality. It must have a New Revelation from God to bring the world's religions into great unity and cooperation, to clarify your understanding of God's Will and Purpose for the world and how God works here, working through individuals from the inside out.

It is being given at a time of great and growing crisis in the world, greater than you now understand. The need is so great. And God's Love has brought a great Revelation here for you and for others. Though not everyone will be able to receive it and accept it, enough must do so for it to change the course of human behavior and understanding.

You can do this because you love God and God loves you. And your bond has never been fully broken. Even though you have chosen to come into Separation and to dwell there, it is still alive and powerful within you. It supersedes your religious beliefs. It is more important than your ideas. It is more powerful than anything that you believe is powerful.

It can reclaim you. It can change your life. It can reunite bonds with others. It can build bridges between nations, built now out of necessity, for humanity must unite to survive in a declining world.

The religions will be continued because they are all important. Do not try to make your own religion, for that is foolish. For God has sent the ladders down into the deep ravine, more than one so that everyone would have a chance to climb out. And now God has sent another ladder down into the ravine because this is required at this time, at a time of Revelation.

A Messenger has been sent from the Angelic Assembly, from which all the Messengers have come. So there can be no real contention between the world's religions, for those who came to bring them all came from the same Source. Half holy, half human they are once they are in the world. They are not gods. For there is no God but God. But they are the most important people in the world for what they have come to give and the great change and benefit they can provide, for this time and for the times to come.

This is your challenge. You must have a change of heart to play your greater part in the world. You must receive Revelation to understand your own religious pathway.

Let God help you now. Let God support the world. God will not take over the world. But God will make you powerful enough and united enough to restore the world and create a future far better than the past, to preserve human freedom and sovereignty in the universe, and give humanity a permanent home here in the world, leading to greater accomplishments and fulfillment, and avoiding the perils of catastrophe.

It is because of the Heart of God that this is being given to you now, that We are speaking to you now and that the Messenger is here now. Understand this, and your life will come into focus. And your heart will grow. Your strength will grow. And the love within you will be released out into the world.

IMPORTANT TERMS

---

*T*he New Message from God reveals that our world stands at the greatest threshold in the history and evolution of humanity. At this threshold, a New Message from God has come. It reveals the great change that is coming to the world and our destiny within the Greater Community of life beyond our world, for which we are unaware and unprepared.

Here the Revelation redefines certain familiar terms, but within a greater context, and introduces other terms that are new to the human family. It is important to understand these terms when reading the texts of the New Message.

GOD is revealed in the New Message as the Source and Creator of all life and of countless races in the universe. Here the greater reality of God is unveiled in the expanded context of all life in this world and all life in the universe. This greater context redefines the meaning of our understanding of God and of God's Power and Presence in our lives. The New Message states that to understand what God is doing in our world, we must understand what God is doing in the entire universe. This understanding is now being revealed for the first time through a New Message from God. In the New Message, God is not a personage or a singular awareness, but instead a pervasive force and reality that permeates all life, existing beyond the limited boundaries of all theology and religious understanding. God speaks to the deepest part of each person through the power of Knowledge that lives within them.

THE SEPARATION is the ongoing state and condition of being separate from God. The Separation began when part of Creation willed to have the freedom to be apart from God, to live in a state of Separation. As a result, God created our evolving world and the expanding universe as a place for the separated to live in countless forms and places. Before the Separation, all life was in a timeless state of pure union. It is to this original state of union with God that all those living in Separation are ultimately called to return—through service, contribution and the discovery of Knowledge. It is God's mission in our world and throughout the universe to reclaim the separated through Knowledge, which is the part of each individual still connected to God.

KNOWLEDGE is the deeper spiritual mind and intelligence within each person, waiting to be discovered. Knowledge represents the eternal part of us that has never left God. The New Message speaks of Knowledge as the great hope for humanity, an inner power at the heart of each person that God's New Message is here to reveal and to call forth. Knowledge exists beyond the intellect. It alone has the power to guide each of us to our higher purpose and destined relationships in life.

THE ANGELIC ASSEMBLY is the great Angelic Presence that watches over the world. This Assembly is part of the hierarchy of service and relationship established by God to oversee the redemption and return of all separate life in the universe. Every world where sentient life exists is watched over by an Angelic Assembly. The Assembly overseeing our world has translated the Will of God for our time into human language and understanding, which is now revealed through the New Message from God. The term Angelic Assembly is synonymous with the terms Angelic Presence and Angelic Host.

THE NEW MESSAGE FROM GOD is an original Revelation and communication from God to the people of the world, both for our time and the times to come. The New Message is a gift from the

Creator of all life to people of all nations and religions and represents the next great expression of God's Will and Plan for the human family. The New Message is over 9000 pages in length and is the largest Revelation ever given to the world, given now to a literate world of global communication and growing global awareness. The New Message is not an offshoot or reformation of any past tradition. It is a New Message from God for humanity, which now faces great instability and upheaval in the world and the great threshold of emerging into a Greater Community of intelligent life in the universe.

THE VOICE OF REVELATION is the united voice of the Angelic Assembly, delivering God's Message through a Messenger sent into the world for this task. Here the Assembly speaks as one Voice, the many speaking as one. For the very first time in history, you are able to hear the actual Voice of Revelation speaking through God's Messenger. It is this Voice that has spoken to all God's Messengers in the past. The Word and the Sound of the Voice of Revelation are in the world anew.

THE MESSENGER is the one chosen, prepared and sent into the world by the Angelic Assembly to receive the New Message from God. The Messenger for this time is Marshall Vian Summers. He is a humble man with no position in the world who has undergone a long and difficult preparation to be able to fulfill such an important role and mission in life. He is charged with a great burden, blessing and responsibility to receive God's pure Revelation and to protect and present it in the world. He is the first of God's Messengers to reveal the reality of a Greater Community of intelligent life in the universe. The Messenger has been engaged in a process of Revelation for over 30 years. He is alive in the world today.

THE PRESENCE can refer to either the presence of Knowledge within the individual, the Presence of the Angelic Assembly or ultimately the Presence of God. The Presence of these three realities offers a life-changing experience of grace and relationship that can be found by following the mystery in life and by studying and practicing either one of God's past Revelations or God's New Revelation for the world. The New Revelation offers a modern pathway to experiencing the power of this Presence in your life.

STEPS TO KNOWLEDGE is an ancient book of spiritual practice now being given by God to the world for the first time. In taking this mysterious journey, each person is led to the discovery of the power of Knowledge and the experience of profound inner knowing, which can lead them to their higher purpose and calling in life.

THE GREATER COMMUNITY is the larger universe of intelligent life in which our world has always existed. This Greater Community encompasses all worlds in the universe where sentient life exists, in all states of evolution and development. The New Message reveals that humanity is in an early and adolescent phase of its development and that the time has now come for humanity to prepare to emerge into the Greater Community. It is here, standing at the threshold of space, that humanity discovers that it is not alone in the universe, or even within its own world.

THE GREATER COMMUNITY WAY OF KNOWLEDGE represents God's Work in the universe, which is to reclaim the separated in all worlds through the power of Knowledge that is inherent in all intelligent life. To understand what God is doing in our world, we must begin to understand what God is doing in the entire universe. For the first time in history, The Greater Community Way of Knowledge is being presented to the world through a New Message from God. The New Message opens the portal to this timeless Work of God underway throughout the Greater Community of life in the universe. We who stand at the threshold of emerging into this Greater

Community must have access to this greater reality and this pathway of redemption in order to understand our future and destiny as a race.

THE GREATER DARKNESS is an Intervention underway by certain races from the Greater Community who are here to take advantage of a weak and divided humanity. This Intervention is occurring at a time when the human family is entering a period of increasing breakdown and disorder, in the face of the Great Waves of change. The Intervention presents itself as a benign and redeeming force while in reality its ultimate goal is to undermine human freedom and self-determination and take control of the world and its resources. The New Message reveals that the Intervention seeks to secretly establish its influence here in the minds and hearts of people at a time of growing confusion, conflict and vulnerability. As the native peoples of this world, we are called upon to oppose this Intervention and to alert and educate others, thus uniting the human family in a great common purpose and preparing our world for the challenges and opportunities of life in the Greater Community.

THE GREAT WAVES OF CHANGE are a set of powerful environmental, economic and social forces now converging upon the world. The Great Waves are the result of humanity's misuse and overuse of the world, its resources and its environment. The Great Waves have the power to drastically alter the face of the world—producing economic instability, runaway climate change, violent weather and the loss of arable land and freshwater resources, threatening to produce a world condition of great difficulty and human suffering. The Great Waves are not an end times or apocalyptic event, but instead a period of transition to a new world condition. The New Message reveals what is coming for the world and the greater preparation that must be undertaken by enough people.

It is calling for human unity and cooperation born now out of sheer necessity for the preservation and protection of human civilization.

HIGHER PURPOSE refers to the specific contribution each person was sent into the world to make and the unique relationships that will enable the fulfillment of this purpose. Knowledge within the individual holds their higher purpose and destiny for them, which cannot be ascertained by the intellect alone. These must be discovered, followed and expressed in service to others to be fully realized. The world needs the demonstration of this higher purpose from many more people as never before.

SPIRITUAL FAMILY refers to the small working groups formed after the Separation to enable all individuals to work towards greater states of union and relationship, undertaking this over a long span of time, culminating in their final return to God. Your Spiritual Family represents the relationships you have reclaimed through Knowledge during your long journey through Separation. Some members of your Spiritual Family are in the world and some are beyond the world. The Spiritual Families are a part of the mysterious Plan of God to free and reunite all those living in Separation.

ANCIENT HOME refers to the reality of life and the state of awareness and relationship you had before entering the world, and to which you will return after your life in the world. Your Ancient Home is a state of connection and relationship with your Spiritual Family, the Assembly and God.

The Messenger

Marshall Vian Summers is the Messenger for the New Message from God. For over three decades he has been the recipient of a vast New Revelation, given to prepare humanity for the great environmental, social and economic changes that are coming to the world and for humanity's emergence into a universe of intelligent life.

In 1981, at the age of 32, Marshall Vian Summers had a direct encounter with the Angelic Presence who had been guiding and preparing him for his future role and calling. This encounter forever altered the course of his life and initiated him into a deeper relationship with the Angelic Assembly, requiring that he surrender his life to God. This began the long, mysterious process of receiving God's New Message for humanity.

Following this mysterious initiation, he received the first revelations of the New Message from God. Over the decades since, a vast Revelation for humanity has unfolded, at times slowly and at times in great torrents. During these long years, he had to proceed with the support of only a few individuals, not knowing what this growing Revelation would mean and where it would ultimately lead.

The Messenger has walked a long and difficult road to receive and present the largest Revelation ever given to the human family. Still today the Voice of Revelation continues to flow through him as he faces the great challenge of bringing God's New Revelation to a troubled and conflicted world.

Read and hear the Story of the Messenger:
www.newmessage.org/story

Hear and watch the world teachings of the Messenger:
www.newmessage.org/messenger

THE VOICE OF REVELATION

For the first time in history, you can hear the Voice of Revelation, such a Voice as spoke to the prophets and Messengers of the past and is now speaking again through a new Messenger who is in the world today.

The Voice of Revelation is not the voice of one individual, but that of the entire Angelic Assembly speaking together, all as one. Here God communicates beyond words to the Angelic Assembly, who then translate God's Message into human words and language that we can comprehend.

The revelations of this book were originally spoken in this manner by the Voice of Revelation through the Messenger Marshall Vian Summers. This process of Divine Revelation has occurred since 1981. The Revelation continues to this day.

The original audio recordings of the Voice of Revelation
are made available to all people.
To hear the Voice, which is the source of
the text contained in this book and throughout
the New Message, please visit:
www.newmessage.org/experience

To learn more about the Voice of Revelation, what it is
and how it speaks through the Messenger, visit:
www.newmessage.org/voiceofrevelation

ABOUT THE SOCIETY FOR THE NEW MESSAGE FROM GOD

Founded in 1992 by Marshall Vian Summers, The Society for the New Message from God is an independent religious 501(c)(3) non-profit organization that is primarily supported by readers and students of the New Message, receiving no sponsorship or revenue from any government or religious organization.

The Society's mission is to bring the New Message from God to people everywhere so that humanity can find its common ground, preserve the Earth, protect human freedom and advance human civilization as we stand at the threshold of great change.

Marshall Vian Summers and The Society have been given the immense responsibility of bringing the New Message into the world. The members of The Society are a small group of dedicated individuals who have committed their lives to fulfill this mission. For them, it is a burden and a great blessing to give themselves wholeheartedly in this great service to humanity.

THE SOCIETY FOR THE NEW MESSAGE

Contact us:

P.O. Box 1724 Boulder, CO 80306-1724
(303) 938-8401 (800) 938-3891
011 303 938 84 01 (International)
(303) 938-1214 (fax)
society@newmessage.org
www.newmessage.org
www.alliesofhumanity.org
www.newknowledgelibrary.org

Connect with us:

www.youtube.com/thenewmessagefromgod
www.facebook.com/newmessagefromgod
www.facebook.com/marshallsummers
www.twitter.com/godsnewmessage

About the Worldwide
Community of the
New Message from God

The New Message from God is being shared by people around the world. Representing more than 90 countries and over 23 languages, a worldwide community of students has formed to receive and study the New Message and to support the mission of the Messenger and The Society.

Learn more about the worldwide community of people who are learning and living the New Message from God and taking the Steps to Knowledge towards a new and inspired life.

Become a part of a worldwide community of people who are pioneering a new chapter in the human experience. The New Message has the power to awaken the sleeping brilliance in people everywhere and bring new inspiration and wisdom into the lives of people from all nations and faith traditions.

Hear the Voice of Revelation speaking directly
on the purpose and importance of the Worldwide Community:
www.newmessage.org/theworldwidecommunity

Learn more about the educational opportunities available in the
Worldwide Community:

Forum - www.newmessage.org/forum
Free School - www.newmessage.org/school
Live Internet Broadcasts and International Events -
www.newmessage.org/events
Annual Encampment - www.newmessage.org/encampment
Online Library and Study Pathway - www.newmessage.org/experience